Charting
School
Change

Charting School Change

Improving the Odds for Successful School Reform

Barbara Stanford

CORWIN PRESS, INC.
A Sage Publications Company
Thousand Oaks, California

For information:

Corwin Press, Inc.
A Sage Publications Company
2455 Teller Road
Thousand Oaks, California 91320
E-mail: order@corwin.sagepub.com

SAGE Publications Ltd.
6 Bonhill Street
London EC2A 4PU
United Kingdom

SAGE Publications India Pvt. Ltd.
M-32 Market
Greater Kailash I
New Delhi 110 048 India

Printed in the United States of America

Library of Congress Cataloging-in-Publication Data

Stanford, Barbara Dodds.
    Charting school change: improving the odds for successful school reform / by Barbara Stanford.
        p. cm.
    Includes bibliographical references and index.
    ISBN 0-8039-6488-9 (cloth: acid-free paper). — ISBN
0-8039-6489-7 (pbk.: acid-free paper)
    1. School management and organization—United States—Planning.
2. Educational change—United States—Planning. 3. Education—
Social aspects—United States. I. Title.
    LB2805.S7435 1998
    371.2′07′0973—dc21   97-45275

This book is printed on acid-free paper.

98 99 00 01 02 03 10 9 8 7 6 5 4 3 2 1

Production Editor: Sherrise M. Purdum
Production Assistant: Denise Santoyo
Editorial Assistant: Kristen L. Gibson
Typesetter/Designer: Rebecca Evans
Indexer: Mary Mortensen
Cover Designer: Marcia M. Rosenburg

Contents

Part II Using Your New Maps to Guide the Change Process

Preface

We educators live in a rapidly changing society. New technology not only offers us new ways of teaching, but it changes the background knowledge our students bring to school and the information available for them to learn. Population changes require us to learn to teach children with different cultural and language backgrounds. Changes in adult lifestyles have removed much of the outside support most of us used to take for granted.

For the past two decades, educators, legislators, parents, and business people have been trying to change schools to adapt to these new conditions. Although there are many models of successful change, those changes have not swept through the majority of public schools. Some reformers are giving up on the public schools and putting their energies into private schools, charter schools, and home schooling.

Charting School Change is a book aimed at the busy professional who wants usable concepts and models. It explains complex theories with simple explanations, diagrams, and examples and gives suggestions for using the theories. Most of the books currently available on school reform and theories of change are in-depth research reports. Readers who are intrigued by the theories introduced here will want to read some of the supporting research listed in the reference section.

Charting School Change is written for teachers, administrators, curriculum specialists, and college faculty who expect to dedicate many years, perhaps a lifetime, to education. Most other books on school change are written for the change agent, a person who has a particular agenda to promote in the schools. *Charting School Change* is written with a longer perspective, for the person who over a career is likely to be in the roles of change agent, change resistor, change preserver, and the target of other change agents.

My first impulse to write this book came from seeing reforms in the 1980s repeating over and over the mistakes we had made—and I thought we had learned from—in the 1960s. However, as I began to gather material for a book, I realized that the problem was not only that educators did not have a good historical memory but that we did not have the mental tools for observing, interpreting, and analyzing our experiences.

I could recount my stories of reform and collapse of reform, and I could sense intuitively when we were repeating errors or failing to take steps that would lead to success, but I did not have a vocabulary or a conceptual framework that I could use to explain the issues even to myself, let alone communicate them to others.

I could recount my personal memories of a dedicated group of teachers at Vashon High School in St. Louis, Missouri, in the 1960s, who were beginning to build parental support and academic quality when political changes swept away many of the achievements, but I had no theoretical framework to explain either our successes or our failures. I could describe the way the faculty of Fairview High School, in Boulder, Colorado, designed a radically new curriculum in the 1970s and the parts of it that failed immediately, the parts that survived for awhile, and the parts that ultimately collapsed. But I had no vocabulary that would let me generalize that experience.

I could also recall the changes of the late 1970s and early 1980s, the "back to basics" movement, that attempted to correct the mistakes of the 1970s but that made the same kinds of mistakes and generated a pendulum swing away from the basics in the mid-1980s. But I did not have a theory that would show a more efficient route to change.

I could go beyond my own experience and collect documentation of the many curriculum and structural experiments of the 1960s, 1970s, and 1980s and their collapses, but without a theoretical framework, they were just a collection of documents.

In 1988, I began working with the Collaboratives for Humanities and Arts Teaching (CHART), a national network of projects jointly supported by the Rockefeller Foundation, local school districts, local humanities institutions, and local funders. Through CHART, I worked intensively with teams of teachers from 25 schools around Arkansas, and I had opportunities for sharing experiences and exploring theories with project directors from around the country and leading researchers and theorists. I found not only more stories of success and failure, but I found people who were developing theoretical models to interpret their experiences.

I also began to see connections to bodies of research that had previously seemed unrelated. In graduate school, I had been introduced to concepts of systems theory by Kenneth and Elise Boulding, who were pioneers in systems theory. They were developing an interdisciplinary program in conflict management and peace studies and stimulated my long-term interest in conflict management in schools. More important, they taught me to look at conflict and change as patterns in complex systems.

The systems models that we were exploring in the early 1970s were quite primitive. I was frustrated that they could not account for transformational change, so I was excited when researchers in apparently unrelated fields, such as chemistry, computer science, and biology, began to develop complex systems models that did.

By now, there is a large body of books on school change ranging from case studies to general theories of change. Most bookstores also have a shelf full of books on general theories of change, chaos, complexity, and restructuring. Systems change, however, is a vast and vital topic that we have only begun to explore.

Charting School Change covers a somewhat different territory than other books on the subject, drawing on experiences in teaching humanities in challenging urban and rural schools. It also builds a unified theory by drawing on a different combination of disciplines than most other books. It includes concepts from conflict management theory and global systems theories not discussed in other books.

Part I of the book explains the need for a new conceptual framework, introduces the basic concepts of self-organizing systems, and shows how these concepts help us to interpret common phenomena in school reform.

Chapter 1, "Changing Maps for a Changing World," explains the reasons our old mental maps are dysfunctional and introduces the basic system concepts of multiple perspectives, the edge of chaos, self-organization, and scale. Chapter 2, "Revising Dysfunctional Maps of the Reform Process," explains why so many promising reforms disappear and why some of the most important changes seem invisible to school reformers. Chapter 3, "Mapping Dangers and Opportunities," explains the mechanism by which systems transform themselves and provides tools for reformers to recognize both dangers and opportunities.

Part II is a practical handbook for applying systems concepts to specific dimensions of school change. Each chapter looks at a specific part of the change process from a self-organizing-system perspective and offers practical suggestions.

Chapter 4, "Developing a Vision in a World You Don't Own," provides suggestions for vision setting in a complex, changing world of multiple perspectives. Chapter 5, "Building a Knowledge Base for Change," offers a new way of looking at the kinds, amount, and costs of the knowledge needed for change. Chapter 6, "Building Teams and Partnerships," shows how to develop teams around mutual benefit. Chapter 7, "Charting Conflict," shows the important role that conflict plays in systems change and offers suggestions on managing conflict. Chapter 8, "Monitoring Results," examines the need for and the kinds of assessment needed in complex systems.

The final chapter, "Deepening Roots in a Swirling World," shows the need for individuals to connect to culture and tradition during periods of rapid change.

The artwork in this book was drawn by Charles Coleman, an art teacher form Anna Strong Elementary School in Lee County, Arkansas, who was one of the first teachers to join the CHART project in Arkansas. I appreciate the assistance of Walter Nunn, the first director of the Arkansas CHART project, the CHART directors from all of the projects, and the CHART teachers who inspired this book.

About the Author

Barbara Stanford is Assistant Professor in the College of Education at the University of Arkansas at Little Rock. She first began exploring the ideas in this book as a teacher at Vashon High School in St. Louis, Missouri, where she discovered the need for a multicultural curriculum, and at Fairview High School in Boulder, Colorado, where she first participated in school restructuring. Her first publications, *Black Literature for High School Students* (National Council of Teachers of English), *Developing Effective Classroom Groups*, and *Myths and Modern Man*, came from her classroom experiences.

While completing her PhD at the University of Colorado, she encountered concepts and problems of complex systems from Kenneth Boulding, Elise Boulding, the World Order Models Project, and others who were struggling with ways of conceptualizing international and interpersonal conflict management.

She was Director of the Arkansas project of the Collaboratives for Humanities and Arts Teaching (CHART) from 1989 to 1995.

Part One

Charting the Change Process

Have you ever set out with a map to find a new destination only to discover that a new superhighway cut across the map you were following or that a road had been closed or a highway rerouted or that a whole new subdivision was there in front of you but not on your map? With an out-of-date map, you probably lost a lot of time if you made it to your destination at all.

Those of us who have been involved in school change have had many such experiences of frustration and anxiety as we have followed the clearly marked maps of consultants and researchers toward school reform but have found that our territory did not match the maps.

During the past decade, school territory has been changing as rapidly as roads and subdivision, and we educators have not only had to draw new maps, we have had to develop new kinds of maps that can accommodate the rapid change.

Part I of this book explores the problems with our old maps and the reasons they kept leading us to blind alleys and wasting our time and energy. It introduces a new set of maps that provides a more accurate model of the processes of change. Part II will give you detailed instructions on how to use the new maps.

Chapter One

Changing Maps
for a Changing World

If you are an educator, you are probably involved with change or are the target of someone who wants to change you. Recently, my colleagues and I listed five major changes we were trying to make that semester. We also counted 13 administrators, committees, regulatory agencies, and foundations that were trying to change us in a variety of contradictory directions.

How do we make decisions among all of the ideas, recommendations, proposals, and directives? How do we cope when we don't have the power to make the decisions that we see are needed. What do we do when a state legislature or a principal mandates a change we don't support? How do we handle contradictory instructions from different places on the chain of command?

Are You Frustrated With Change?

If you have been working on school reform for more than 3 years, you may have begun losing confidence in your ability to make decisions. You have probably had problems with your decision-making strategies. You have probably made careful plans but have found that forces beyond your control swept away your results. You may have carefully implemented a program only to find that the results were very different from the ones you expected.

Many educators have become so frustrated with change that they are ready to give up. One teacher friend said yesterday, "I've been through so many change processes, I just turn off when new ideas are brought up." Another colleague said recently, "Everything is such a mess, I'm not going to try to figure it out any more. I'm going to close my door, teach my classes, and go home and enjoy myself."

But change itself is not necessarily frustrating or confusing. Many people, in fact, find change exhilarating. Many of us feel stimulated and excited about creating something new.

Do You Need a New Set of Maps?

After 33 years of working for and studying educational change, including 10 years of participating in a national change project, I am convinced that the deep frustration and sense of powerlessness teachers feel today comes not from change itself but from dysfunctional maps of change. It comes from the dissonance between our mental map of the way the world works and what we see when we try to follow the map.

According to psychologist Jean Piaget's theories, we construct mental maps of our world and how it works. When we map a new experience that does not fit our old maps, we feel contradictions or cognitive dissonance. As cited by Fosnot (1996), the solution is to "construct a new, more encompassing notion that explains and resolves the prior contradictions" (p. 16).

Piaget told us that we construct our maps from our own experiences. However, the processes of change today are so large and so complex that no one individual can see the whole process, and the problems with our maps are so fundamental that we need not a minor adjustment but a completely different kind of map making. Inventing a new type of map making is a bigger task than most teachers have time for in between preparing for class Monday.

This book shares the maps a network of educators developed over a 10-year experiment with change and the maps that I have found in other disciplines that match our experiences.

Why Our Old Maps Are Dysfunctional

If you were educated in American schools, you were carefully trained in a way of mapping the world. These maps were based on the theories of mathematicians and scientists that the physical world could be mapped mathematically. They assumed that the physical world worked like a clock or a machine and that they could discover the laws by which it worked. These mathematical, mechanical maps spurred the scientific and industrial revolutions, which have changed our physical lives.

By the time we were educated, mathematical and mechanical maps so dominated our thinking that we were taught to map human behavior and schools in the same way. We learned to map problems by breaking them down into their parts. We learned to map cause-and-effect relationships. We learned that the shortest distance between two points is a straight line—both in geometry and in school change. We learned to map intelligence with IQ scores and learning with percentage grades.

However, our experience and the experience of most reformers who have been involved in school change for more than 5 years is that these maps do not work in school change. When we use mechanical, mathematical maps to look at complex systems such as schools and to plot a route to change, we make the wrong choices, we go in the wrong directions, and we miss opportunities. We head for destinations that do not exist over roads that are not there, and we miss the shortcuts and mountain passes that lead us to real destinations.

This book presents a new way of mapping the route to change. As Renate and Geoffrey Caine (Caine & Caine, 1997) write, in *Education on the Edge of Possibility,*

> We are leaving behind one way of looking at the world—a way that is built on a belief in stability and controlled change as ideal. In its place, we're moving toward an emerging understanding of the dynamism of life at every level. (p. 10)

Learning to Think About Change

The map of change presented here grew out of my experiences with a group of educators who participated in a 10-year experiment in school change. It is not about the changes we made in our schools. It is about something more important: the changes we made in the ways we think about schools and change. It tells how we revised our mental maps of change, both through our own explorations and through learning from concepts and models developed by others. It shares the new maps, concepts, and process .descriptions that we found useful and suggests ways for you to use them.

The Collaboratives for Humanities and Arts Teaching (CHART) is a national network of urban and rural projects designed to improve teaching in the humanities and the arts for average students. From 1984 to 1995, 16 projects were funded by the Rockefeller Foundation in collaboration with local funders. Some of the projects had a short life span, whereas others continue today with other funding. However, the life span of the projects was not nearly as important as the role the CHART projects played in developing new ways of mapping complexity and change.

The following chapters present not only the maps that we developed but the experiences that led us to those maps. Most of us learn new maps better from stories than from abstract concepts and theories.

Mapping Skill #1: Learning to Use Multiple Perspectives

The first new mapping skill that most CHART members learned was the basic concept that the world can be mapped in a variety of ways. We learned to view the world from multiple perspectives. Because CHART projects focused on multicultural and international curricula, most of us first began developing new mental maps when we confronted another culture.

Learning Multiple Perspectives in Another Culture

The Arkansas CHART project began with a seminar in Guadalajara, Mexico, on Mexican culture. Teams of teachers from eight schools went to the seminar with clear maps of their goals. They were going to learn Mexican history, literature, art, and music, and they were going to add the new information to their courses at home.

Most of the teachers were from isolated rural communities and had had little contact with other cultures. They packed their American maps of the way the world works along with their clothes. They quickly realized that they had to learn new geographical and language maps to function in a city with a larger population than the entire state of Arkansas.

It took a little longer to learn that they needed new cultural maps. They were introduced to the concepts of Mexican cultural maps by a panel of faculty at the Autonomous University of Guadalajara. The panel emphasized the differences in the ways the two cultures map time.

They explained that in the United States, time is perceived as a simple, uninteresting, mechanical concept going in a straight line of progress by intervals equally marked off. Time is used or saved, and its value is measured in accomplishments that lead toward progress. Mexican maps of time are multidimensional, including endless cycles of the seasons of nature; the movement of the planets, the sun, and the moon; the ceremonies of the Christian liturgical year; the ceremonies of the Aztec and Mayan cyclical calendars—all present in the eternal now. The value of time is the richness of the present moment.

Professor Romo de la Rosa compared a Mexican and an American in a business meeting. The American's mind is mentally ticking off the clock and going through items on a preset agenda. The Mexican's mind is looking for clues about the development of a relationship that must be formed before business plans have any meaning (see Figure 1.1).

Professor Mario Martín showed us how multiple concepts of time shape the structure of the novels, *The Death of Artemio Cruz* (Fuentes, 1991) and *The Underdogs* (Azuela, 1992), and how manipulations of time create the atmosphere of magical realism. Professor Marta Heredia showed us how the past and the present interact in the Day of the Dead celebration and folkloric dance. She also mapped for us the elements in music that Mexicans listen for and the relationship between music, dance, history, and geography.

The concepts did not completely make sense, however, until one day, we were sitting at a restaurant during the noon meal. We had finished our meal, and several members of the group were waiting in growing annoyance for the waiter to bring the check. At last, one of the Mexican professors said,

> You know, it would be extremely rude for the waiter to bring the check before you asked for it. He assumes that you want to relax and enjoy the company of your friends, the music, and the lovely

Figure 1.1.

setting. What do you have to get done that is any more important than the people you are sitting with?

We all smiled sheepishly—and suddenly the whole world looked different. We relaxed and began to flow with the Mexican rhythm of the day. We experienced a different set of priorities. We began to see opportunities to enjoy relationships or beautiful surroundings where before, we had seen obstacles to efficiency.

We soon learned that Mexicans map many dimensions of the world differently than we do and that we could not understand their political systems, their families, and their arts unless we understood their maps. When we looked at their political system through our maps, we were completely puzzled by the choices made by Mexican voters. Those choices made sense when we understood their historical and cultural perspective.

When we recognized that Mexicans map the world differently than we do and that we could not understand their world without understanding their maps, we began to look at some of our other maps differently. We began to map our curricula differently because we realized that we could not teach Mexican art, history, and literature well without teaching basic Mexican cultural maps, and we began to realize that it did not make sense to teach each of the subjects separately.

Learning to Explore Change
Through Multiple Perspectives

More important than our specific cultural maps was the basic concept of multiple perspectives. We now recognized that it is possible to map the world in a number of different ways and that different maps serve different functions. We recognized that when things are not working the way we expect them to, the problem may not be in the world but in our maps.

This concept contradicted a basic tenet that we had been taught from elementary school through university: the concept of the *objective observer.*

We had all been taught that if we used scientific techniques of observation and mathematical precision, we could see the world exactly as everyone else did.

With the concept of multiple perspectives, we realized that in our complex, multicultural world, not only was it impossible for everyone to see exactly the same thing but that we had much more information if we could see the system from a variety of perspectives. If we could not see something important from one map, we learned that we could draw a map from a different perspective.

Mapping Skill #2: Mapping Change on the Edge of Chaos

When our teachers returned from Mexico, they began making changes in their schools. The first year, all eight teams integrated international components into their curricula in exciting ways. But the second year, every one of the teams ran into unexpected problems. At first, each team's problems seemed unique. A supportive principal resigned. A key team member became sick. A school failed to live up to its commitment to provide release time because of unexpected budget cuts.

However, as CHART team members got together on the city or state level and as CHART directors met nationally, we began to discover that such problems in the second year of a project were not the exception but the normal pattern.

The further we got into the process of change, the more contradictions we found between what our mental maps predicted and what actually happened. We began to realize that our maps of the change process worked well when we were making small changes in a stable system, but they seemed to lead us in the wrong directions as we tried to develop interdisciplinary programs that affected the whole school.

As I became more and more convinced that there was a problem in our map of change just as there had been a problem in our maps of Mexican culture, I started looking for a guide, for mapmakers who had already charted the kinds of changes we were trying to make.

The maps of change I found most useful came from two surprising sources: from the writings of a Nobel Prize-winning chemist, Ilya Prigogine, and from books by and about a group of scientists connected with Santa Fe Institute.

Each of these scientists independently developed similar maps of complex change, and the main patterns of their maps fit very well the patterns of change I was seeing in the CHART projects. Their systems seemed far removed from schools. Prigogine studied chemical solutions. Per Bak studied the physics of sandpiles. Stuart Kauffman was working on a new model of biological evolution. Brian Archer studied economic trends. What surprised me was that they had all developed similar maps—and that the maps seemed to fit what I was seeing in CHART.

Part of the reason we could not design our own new maps was that we were looking at our complex system from too short a time perspective, and we were looking at too small a piece of it. Per Bak writes "Complex behavior, whether in geophysics or biology, is always created by a long process of evolution. It cannot be understood by studying the systems with a time frame that is short compared with this evolutionary process" (Bak, 1996, p. 31). Because Bak and Prigogine (Gregoire & Prigogine, 1989) were studying small-scale systems and Kauffman (as cited in Waldrop, 1992) was studying the history of evolution, they could see the whole process, whereas we could see only a small piece of it.

Distinguishing Order, Complexity, and Disorder

A key feature of all of these scientists' maps was the way they mapped the relationship of order, complexity, and disorder.

Prigogine and the Santa Fe scientists divided the world into three states or conditions. Under stable conditions, the world can be mapped the way we were trained to map it. The laws of chemistry, physics, and astronomy that we learned in school, work. The planning strategies that we learned in education courses in college work reasonably well. Reasonably clear cause-and-effect relationships can be seen. Most observers will see approximately the same thing. A person can plan a course of action, and the results will be what is expected.

Under conditions of complete disorder or chaos, nothing is predictable. (Note: Some scientists, such as those described in James Glieck's [1987] *Chaos*, have given the term *chaos* or *deterministic chaos* a different meaning.)

Ilya Prigogine won the Nobel Prize for mapping a third domain: far from equilibrium, or as Kauffman put it, on the edge of chaos.

Complex Systems Emerge on the Edge of Chaos

Prigogine discovered that under certain conditions, conditions far from equilibrium, a kind of order could be created that was very different from the order that was described by traditional chemistry and physics.

In this domain on the edge of chaos, a spontaneous order sometimes developed that was very different from structures scientists had previously described. Structures on the edge of chaos exist by manipulating the laws of chemistry and physics and creating a domain that operates by laws that are different from those outside the system. For example, the second law of thermodynamics says that all complex systems slowly break down and become less ordered. However, self-organizing systems consume energy from their environment, so they grow ever more complex while their environment continues to break down. Living things on planet earth consume energy from the sun, which enables them to grow ever more complex structures that exist nowhere else in the universe, even though astronomers tell us that the sun and the solar system are on a long, slow road to destruction (Prigogine, Gregoire, & Babloyants, 1972a).

Mitchell Waldrop (1992), in his book, *Complexity*, which focuses on the research of the Santa Fe group, states,

> These complex systems have somehow acquired the ability to bring order and chaos into a special kind of balance. This balance point—often called the edge of chaos—is where the components of a system never quite lock into place, and yet never quite dissolve into turbulence, either. The edge of chaos is where life has enough stability to sustain itself and enough creativity to deserve the name of life. The edge of chaos is where new ideas and innovative genotypes are forever nibbling away at the edges of the status quo. . . . The edge of chaos is the constantly shifting battle zone between stagnation and anarchy, the one place where a complex system can be spontaneous, adaptive, and alive. (Waldrop,1992, p. 12)

CHART Teachers Explore the Edge of Chaos

CHART leaders did not map the edge of chaos in the kind of detail that these scientists did, but when we read their concepts, they matched our experience.

CHART deliberately chose to work in urban and rural schools, the schools most affected by areas of breakdown in our society. These were the schools that many parents and teachers were fleeing. Order was breaking down, and old methods were not working. But we found that these were the schools where we had the best chance of starting something new. Schools where the old methods were working were not interested, and schools that had collapsed too far simply consumed resources with no results. We recognized the edge of chaos as the best place for reform.

In addition, we reflected that the teaching methods we promoted brought the classroom to the edge of chaos. We discovered that the best humanities classes were somewhat unpredictable, uncontrollable, and a bit dangerous, but they did not disintegrate into disorder. The best classes stayed on the edge between order and control and chaos. As Judith Rényi (quoted in Beard, 1992) summarized CHART director's journals, "A lot of you talked about good classroom teaching being moments when you're not doing what's comfortable, but when you're pushing the students 'off the path' " (p. 193).

The best teachers, we all agreed, kept their classes between traditional order and chaos and developed a sophisticated, complex order that encouraged the emergence of new ideas and patterns of collaboration and problem solving.

We also recognized that our projects worked best on the edge of chaos, with a certain amount of freedom from traditional school structures but without collapsing into chaos. In our final national directors' meeting, we shared our experiences in pushing school systems to the edge of chaos. Most of us had found that we could make small-scale changes without much problem but that when we tried to push larger system change, we found ourselves on unfamiliar territory. Several of us recalled choosing to step back into the safety zone, and even after 10 years, we were not sure whether we had made the best choice when we stayed in the safety zone or when we pushed into the edge of chaos.

The maps of Prigogine, Kauffman, and Bak confirmed our instincts and reflection that we had to go to the edge of chaos to get the kinds of changes we wanted, but once we had gotten there, we had no maps to guide our steps.

Mapping Skill #3:
Understanding Self-Organization

By the time most of us had been involved with CHART for 3 or 4 years, we knew that we needed new maps, but none of us had the perspective, time, or perhaps the intellectual power to map what happens on the edge of chaos. Ilya Prigogine won a Nobel Prize for mapping these processes.

Prigogine mapped the order that emerges on the edge of chaos as self-organizing systems. There, order, he said, does not grow out of an external plan. There is no central control and no lines of authority. Unlike mechanical systems, they have no external designer or maker. The system emerges when each individual component of the system has enough freedom to make choices but enough structure that the choices form patterns.

The shape and patterns of the larger system come from the components making constant "decisions" based on information and communication with other parts of the system. Patterns emerge because each of the components makes decisions based on information about the larger system and the other components.

No entity in the system is completely free, because all decisions are based on a repertoire of possible responses to different conditions and information from the environment about those conditions. A self-organizing system is never completely predictable because it can exist only if there are choices, but it is not completely unpredictable because, to exist, there must be patterns in the choices.

One of the simplest examples described by Prigogine of a self-organizing system was a chemical solution that created elaborate designs as the component molecules switched from one state to another. He found that individual molecules switched their state in response to the neighboring molecule's state. The exact design was never predictable, but the general pattern could be predicted.

Prigogine also used the model to study traffic patterns, looking for patterns in changing conditions that changed people's driving decisions. For example, on my usual route to work, if the entrance ramp to the highway is backed up to a certain point, cars will start getting out of the entrance ramp lane and start heading for the route to downtown over regular streets.

We all have the freedom to choose from a number of routes, but most of us are responding to time pressure and make our judgment on which will be the quicker route. If one route is blocked, many of us make similar judgments about what new route will be faster (Gregoire & Prigogine, 1989).

Mapping Schools as Self-Organizing Systems

Mapping schools as self-organizing systems changes our focus from regulations, visions, and directives to individual decision making.

CHART educators did not develop the concept of self-organizing systems independently, but we gradually shifted our focus from a traditional emphasis on organizational charts to treating each individual as a decision maker.

At first, we followed the traditional chain of command as we tried to find who had the power to make changes. In an urban school district, we could spend months going from the department chair to the principal to the director of secondary curriculum to the associate superintendent for curriculum to the superintendent to the school board. Frequently, by the time we got through the chain, at least one key person had moved, died, resigned, or retired. Furthermore, we discovered that every person in the chain could block change, but none of them had the power to implement the kinds of changes we wanted.

We learned from experience to look at each individual in the chain as a decision maker. Most were influenced by the chain of command, but almost everyone made decisions based on several sources of information. If teachers thought that principals' suggestions or directives were unwise, they had many ways to sabotage them.

The old maps with long paper trails of regulations and curriculum usually had little relationship to what was actually going on in classrooms. The decisions teachers made about whether or how to implement written directives were what shaped the real system.

Mapping Skill #4: Finding the Right Scale

As I began to study complex adaptive systems maps, I realized that much of our confusion and many of our poor predictions came from looking at schools on too small a map. To see the emergence of order on the edge of chaos or to understand the concepts of self-organization, I had to borrow maps from people who could see the processes of change on a larger scale. To understand the changes happening in schools or to make effective changes, we had to map schools in on a larger map of our whole society.

The complex systems that Prigogine and others discovered on the edge of chaos were not independent systems. They were systems within systems within systems.

Nobel Prize-winning physicist Murray Gell Mann (as quoted in Lewin, 1992), says that complex adaptive systems "are pattern seekers. . . . They interact with the environment, 'learn' from the experience, and adapt as a result" (p. 15).

Our traditional maps looked at the school as if it were an independent system. Complex adaptive system maps show that complex systems on the edge of chaos cannot be understood independently of their environment. Their shape is a response to the environment, and they in turn shape their environment.

No single observer can see a complex human system from all of the perspectives we need to see to understand it. We need to be able to see the system in relation to the larger systems of which it is a part, and we need to be able to see the smaller systems that are its components. Shifting from a small-scale perspective to a large-scale perspective often clears up mysteries.

Mapping School Change on
Maps of Planetary Change

The changes CHART was trying to make in schools can be mapped as part of the efforts of the human species to adapt to the global changes of the late 20th century. CHART programs were a response to two national and probably global trends that affected our schools: shifting demographics and changing institutions. The ways teachers adapted to these changes affected the ways other parts of society needed to shift. CHART educators threw their efforts into changing schools in ways that would affect the way the society as a whole adapted.

Adapting to Changing Demographics by
Creating a Multicultural Community

CHART's stated focus was to improve teaching in the humanities. CHART was started from outside the schools by a foundation that was concerned that young people were not making the connections to arts and humanities institutions that previous generations had. The most obvious problem was that a larger percentage of the younger generation was of African American, Latin American, and Asian descent, and the humanities texts they were being introduced to were primarily European.

As CHART evolved, it solved the problem by expanding the range of humanities texts students encountered and by developing skills in interpreting texts from other cultures.

Miami, Florida, was one of the sites where the population was most multicultural and was changing most rapidly. The Dade County Public Schools, the nation's fourth largest school system, is 45% Hispanic, 33% African American, 21% European American, and 1% other. Students enrolled in Dade County schools in the 1990s represented over 124 countries, and more than 30% of the students were born outside the United States (Inhabiting Other Lives, c. 1992).

Ruth Shack (1992), Director of the Dade Community Foundation, welcomed the CHART directors to a conference in 1992 saying, Miami "is a wonderful place to visit, it's so close to the United States" (p. 5). She went on,

> We have for generations used the food metaphor when we talk about bringing people together. Everyone knows about the "melting pot." We talk about the "beef stew," which is a step back from that. Now we've begun talking about the "salad bowl." But I can tell you that I describe Miami as a "TV dinner," with the three pots on the plate with the aluminum barriers. How we get from one side of the barrier to the other is the challenge that this community has not yet learned, but it's something we are working on. (Shack, 1992, p. 7)

CHART worked on that problem with a program called "Inhabiting Other Lives." When I visited Southwest Miami High School to observe the program, students in the computer class were practicing data processing by typing papers on their family histories. Maria was born in Venezuela, but she had lived in Chile and Panama before coming to Miami. Elizabeth came from Cuba. Christian was born in Nicaragua, but his grandfather had come there from the United States to look for gold. Lorena's parents were from Argentina, but her grandfather was from Italy. Ingrid was born in Boston with parents from Guatemala and the Dominican Republic. Lisa, one of the few born in Miami, was of Irish ancestry. Students who spoke English well were given extra credit for helping those who did not.

Down the hall, a social studies class was debating policies toward Haitian immigrants. The discussion was heated because almost a third of the students in the class were themselves immigrants.

"There are too many immigrants here," said T. R. "Everywhere you go, people are speaking Spanish. You can't get a job if you don't speak Spanish."

"People that want to speak English can move somewhere else!" J. S. retorted. "Maybe Minneapolis."

The discussion hovered between hostility and humor. The teacher had clearly trained the group in debate techniques, and he carefully guided students in the difference between open expression of ideas and insult and disrespect. Yet civility and skillful debate techniques could not guarantee a mutually acceptable solution, because it was obvious that the students were aware that the issue they were debating was about the power to control the future of their community and the structure of access to resources.

Demographic predictions suggest that trends now visible in the Miami schools will become national trends. The children that are now in the schools will become the workforce of the next decades, and all institutions will have to make the adjustments that the schools are making today. In 1990, *Time* magazine predicted that by 2056, non-Hispanic whites may be a minority group. According to their predictions, by the year 2020, nonwhite and Hispanic populations will have doubled, whereas the white population will not be increasing (Henry, 1990, p. 28).

Demographic changes affected CHART classrooms, but the choices made by CHART teachers will affect the larger society. The ways young people learn to deal with each other and with their history and their culture will affect the choices they make when their generation controls the political and economic structures of our nation. CHART started from concerns by humanities institutions about the way children were being shaped, but the choices teachers make will affect many other dimensions of society.

Responding to a Disintegrating Support System for Children

A second major national change that stimulated the development of CHART was the disintegration of support for children from the family, community, and government. The schools in which CHART chose to work tended to be in neighborhoods on the edge of chaos.

Assistant Principal John Ignacio, in an interview with Ron Javers, described the situation at Balboa High School in San Francisco, California, a rather typical CHART school:

> This is supposed to be a neighborhood high school, but we have an incredible number of behavior problems. It's really sort of a dumping ground for kids who don't select other magnet schools. . . . Half of our ninth graders don't make it to the tenth in a year. They drop out or move away. These kids are moving all the time; every time their parents have a shot at a better apartment or a slightly safer neighborhood, they move. Our aim is to get them to stay in the same school and graduate with their classmates. We're trying to provide some stability.
>
> There are two pupil profiles, really. One is the kids who come from solid families. They're average kids and they do pretty well. . . . The other group is the kids who we don't really know where they live, or with whom. Some live in garages. These are families who are really struggling. They have tremendous problems. (Javers, 1994, p. 25)
>
> Do you know how hard it is even to find many parents? We have computerized lists of families' names, addresses, and phone numbers. But half the time when you dial the number listed, it's no longer the number. We had a budget to mail fliers and to make phone calls, but many times we simply couldn't make contact. Other times parents chose not to come to meetings. Those community people who did get involved were often not parents, but community activists. (Javers, 1994, p. 27)

The changes in U.S. society of the last two decades have benefited some sectors of society, but they have been disastrous for many children. Psychologist James Comer (1992) states,

> Prior to 1945 we were a nation of small towns and rural areas. Children grew up in environments that could be termed—in the very best sense of the word—predictable. Their surroundings were populated by familiar adults—parents, relatives, neighbors, clergy, and other authority figures—who spoke a common language about expected behavior. The regular social interactions among those adults functioned as a network, enclosing

the children within a consistent value system. Children knew
what to expect from these important adults, who conspired to
assure that their young people grew up to become responsible
citizens of the community and of society. This created a sense of
place, of belonging. (p. A-1)

Comer says that there was an adult conspiracy to keep children
within social boundaries. It was not an ideal world, and many children were not well cared for, but they were the exception rather than
the rule.

Today, many children have limited attention from adults, and
the adults they interact with often come from different cultures and
have antagonistic values. Television provides the only consistent
voice—and its seductive voice promoting material possessions and
the power of violence and exhibiting unhealthy relationships contra-
dicts the weak voices from home and school and possibly church.
Finally, the peer culture takes over.

Our restructured society does not provide children with the kind
of support, role models, and guidance that they need for healthy development. Children come to school with less preparation, but
schools must prepare them for more complex tasks on graduation.
As a result, schools are dealing with children whose needs are much
greater than they were a few years ago.

The Role of the School
in a Changing World

Our nation today is in a state of rapid change. Technology, culture, and knowledge no longer function the way they did in 1980.
These changes were not desired or produced by the public schools.
The crisis in education is not a crisis brought on by the incompetence
of educators. The crisis in education was created by changes in the
world that require humans to invent new ways of thinking and behaving. Schools need to play a key role in guiding those changes.

Schools are being drawn to the edge of chaos by children who
are not only refusing to be shaped into patterns that do not fit the
modern world but who do not have the information or the wisdom
to shape themselves. The challenge of discovering a way to organize
our culture in a world without our traditional boundaries is one of

the major challenges of the late 20th century. A boundaryless society is not complexity but chaos. To avoid collapse, we must design new boundaries.

What is at stake is not something peripheral to our lives. Our cultural values and institutions control the distribution of every kind of power. Cultural images of what makes an ideal man or woman, and what is right and just, play a powerful role in people's decisions about whose authority or domination to accept or challenge. Cultural images shape a woman's decision about whether she should respond to sexual advances from her boss by staying at home and avoiding outside employment, sleeping with him, or suing him for sexual harassment. Cultural images shape a child's decision about whether to invest time in studying science or playing basketball. Cultural images shape a people's decisions about whether to accept unjust conditions, work for political change, or riot.

In many contemporary trends, schools are the front lines of change. Demographic changes affect the schools 15 years before they begin to affect the workplace. Schools have first contact with the generation that grew up with computers, one-parent families. Our society assigned schools the task of integration, which the rest of society was unwilling to tackle. By default, schools are also left on the front lines to deal with most other social adjustments required by new technology.

Teachers are the pioneers who must invent solutions to problems that human beings have never successfully solved in the past. They must educate children to be able to work together in more complex ways with people from a wide range of cultures with instant means of communication. The survival of human society depends on their success.

Our chances of success are much better if we are using the right maps.

Chapter Two

Revising Dysfunctional Maps of the Reform Process

If you have been involved in school change for more than 3 years, you have probably experienced at least one of the following mysteries: the mystery of the missing reforms or the mystery of the invisible reforms.

The Mystery of the Missing Reforms

Hundreds of thousands of teachers have implemented school reform programs in the past decade. I would estimate that CHART was responsible for over 5,000 teachers making significant changes in their classrooms. Today, however, there are probably fewer than a hundred schools where one can see a clear example of a functioning CHART model.

In the hundreds of other school reform models, the problem is similar. Many teachers initially implement reforms, but the percentage of reforms that last for 5 years is quite low. In an informal conversation, Judith Rényi (personal communication, c. 1994), the Director of CHART, once said, "Most school systems chew up innovative projects and spit them out."

There seemed to be some invisible force in school districts that eliminated reforms.

The Mystery of the Invisible Reforms

Not all of the CHART reforms have disappeared. Many are not only still there but have spread far beyond the original CHART schools. However, they are invisible on our traditional maps of change.

The first year they implemented projects, CHART teachers expressed the frustration that their projects seemed to be invisible. They could see students functioning on a much higher level. I could see the significant questions students were asking, the quality of research they were doing in the library, and the motivation to pursue long-term projects.

Teachers complained that their principals evaluated the classes on the state-mandated observation instrument and saw only that the objectives were not written on the board and that the lesson lacked closure or that students were noisy and not in their seats. Thoughtfulness, creativity, depth, and enthusiasm were invisible on the state observation instruments.

As the projects continued, they were imitated by teachers outside the project or they developed in directions not predicted in our proposals. When I visited some communities, I could find CHART-inspired innovations throughout the entire district and sometimes in the community. But when we prepared our report to the Rockefeller Foundation, there was no place to put these changes. Much of the impact of CHART seemed to be invisible.

The mystery of the missing reforms and the resistance of schools to change has been a major theme of educational research of the last decade. Seymour Sarason (1989), in the *Predictable Failure of School Reform*, described a school culture that resists reform. In his book, *The New Meaning of Educational Change*, Michael Fullan (1992) describes hundreds of ways school reform can go awry.

At a 1995 meeting, members of the National Governors' Association generally conceded that their efforts at reform had failed, and guest speaker, IBM Chief Executive Louis Gerstner (as quoted in Kiely, 1995), urged the governors "to confront and expel the people and organizations that are throwing up roadblocks" (p. A7).

Roadblocks or Bad Maps

On our traditional maps to reform, we constantly found roadblocks, and we assumed that someone or some group was deliberately blocking our way. Our old mechanical, mathematical maps generally misinterpreted the blocks and failed to show the superhighways to change that went around them. Furthermore, they mapped the destination of change incorrectly, so we kept looking for destinations that did not exist and failed to recognize the achievements that we had made.

Analyzing Change Efforts
on the Old Maps

Perryville is a very small district in a beautiful rural area of Arkansas. It was one of the first districts in the state to respond to Governor Clinton's proposals for change in the late 1980s, and it participated actively in the state department of education's restructuring program, CHART, and the Coalition of Essential Schools. Perryville had a very good faculty, and they invested heavily in training, team building, and community partnerships. They did everything that the best reform guides of the late 1980s said should be done.

Their results were dramatic. By the early 1990s, visitors were coming from Japan, Senegal, Egypt, and Russia as well as from all over the country to see working models of the most advanced school reforms. Visitors could see high-quality examples of cooperative learning, interdisciplinary instruction, Socratic discussion, student-centered decision making, and portfolio assessment. This all-white southern community also had a model international and multicultural curriculum.

Student results were impressive. Students improved their scores on standardized tests, they attended school more regularly and behaved better when they were there, and many more students were going to college. Special education students were writing research papers, and average students were using the Internet to access a nearby college library 5 years before most other schools in the state.

The process of restructuring was well planned. The program was first introduced in the ninth grade, then expanded to the tenth. It was next adopted by the junior high, followed by the elementary school. Eleventh and twelfth grade teachers were slowly converted to similar methods. Parents were heavily involved in the program, and the whole faculty went on retreats together.

Today, not even a cemetery marker remains to show that those reforms ever existed. Except for two classes, the district has reverted back to its old, traditional form. The "fittest" did not survive.

As soon as the program started, there were conflicts. Parents protested dirty words in one of the literature books and objected to the new grading system. The first principal left in the middle of the first year, and three teachers involved in the program left, partly due to conflict with the new principal. The new principal, however, was committed to the program and hired teachers who were skilled in the new strategies.

Even though the program demonstrated success on test scores and increased the number of students going to college, community resistance grew. A local church was connected with a national organization that publicized their analysis of contradictions between their religion and the Coalition of Essential Schools. Rumors grew. The superintendent left for another district. The principal and key teachers soon followed.

The longer CHART was in existence, the more familiar this story became. Reforms that had spread through schools, districts, and even states slowly eroded or were swept aside by a new reform effort or collapsed when key people resigned or died. Districts that gained national prominence with well-documented successes faced community opposition or district power struggles. Even when reforms were written into state guidelines, they were frequently repealed by the next administration.

Although the rest of the world was undergoing breathtaking change, American schools seemed to have an incredible power to resist all changes. In frustration, educators blamed themselves or someone else, poured more money and resources into the change process, or gave up.

Analyzing Change Efforts on Complex System Maps

If we map the story as a complex system, we start with a larger map. We recognize that the story does not start with Perryville but with the larger systems of which Perryville is a part. And we see different problems and different results.

In the 1980s, the United States was changing rapidly. The institutions such as the church and the family were losing their influence over young people, and the media and peer culture were gaining power. Demographic changes were shifting power from whites to growing minorities. Technology and economic pressures were stimulating changes in the lifestyle of even isolated rural communities.

The system was being drawn to the edge of chaos. Old ways of doing things were no longer working. Parents who raised their children the same way their parents had, found that the children turned out different. Educators who taught as they had been taught found their students unprepared for the jobs of the 1980s.

Economic and political power were shifting, not only within America but between America and other countries. Moral and ethical boundaries were also shifting.

As they found the conditions around them changing, individuals and groups within the self-organizing system began to change their behaviors.

One group of teachers and administrators responded by joining the CHART project and the Coalition of Essential Schools. They gathered innovations from all over the country and built working models of them in Arkansas. They played a major role in building a new knowledge base among Arkansas educators.

Within 5 years, the innovations that Perryville pioneered became widespread throughout the state. It is hard to trace the role Perryville played in the spread of knowledge, for within a few years, the ideas that had seemed so radical in Perryville were common knowledge if not universal practice. But certainly, a large percentage of the teachers who adopted new methods first saw a convincing, working model from a presentation of the Perryville program. Other schools also learned from the mistakes the Perryville team made.

The CHART team was not the only group responding to change. A group of religious leaders focused their attention on different dimensions of society that were changing and experimented with different solutions. From their perspective, the most significant changes were the breakdown of the family and of the traditional values that held society together. They perceived the CHART reforms as encouraging students to question religious values. Their goal was not children who could collaborate in a multicultural world but children who would maintain a lifestyle that conformed to the Word of God.

The more successful the CHART project became as a model of multicultural collaboration, the more of a threat it became to those who wanted to preserve (or create) a Christian, family-centered structure to society and the more it drew attacks from groups in the larger society with a different political agenda.

Both the CHART teachers and the religious group became involved with state and national political actions. One of the CHART teachers left the school to become state coordinator for the Coalition of Essential Schools.

Although visitors to Perryville can no longer see a specific CHART model, they can see examples of the new ideas in almost any school in the state, and they can hear debate on the issues of multiculturalism, collaboration, and restructuring on all levels of society throughout the nation.

The story of Perryville, on a complex systems map, is not the story of one set of reforms in one school district, but it is the story of a planet in change and the role played by one set of pioneers in shaping the direction of our response.

Exploring Resistance to Change in Theories of Complex Systems

We can get a more detailed understanding and more accurate predictions of resistance to change and invisible change by using maps developed by scientists exploring self-organizing systems in other disciplines.

The ways complex systems resist change have recently been studied in fields as unrelated as wind turbulence, weather, evolution, computer simulation, and ecology (Briggs & Peat, 1989). Researchers are finding that a certain kind of resistance to change seems to be a universal, defining, essential characteristic of self-organizing or complex adaptive systems.

Self-organizing systems are not completely stable or unchanging. They are, as described in Chapter 1, made up of the individual decisions made by their components. However, they are capable of maintaining their shapes and of even restoring after large disruptions. Prigogine noted that as long as conditions remain stable, self-organizing systems can absorb major disruptions and reconstruct themselves (Gregoire & Prigogine, 1989). Because a self-organizing system emerges from the choices of its components, as long as similar components are responding to similar information, the system will remain stable and will reconstruct itself after major disruptions.

For example, if we think of a school as a building, it can be completely destroyed by fire or hurricane or tornado. However, if we think of a school as a system of individuals following patterns of interaction, we can see that within a week after the building is destroyed, most schools are functioning again in a different space. Eventually, a newer building will replace the old one, and the human system may be organized a little differently, but much of the activity will continue unchanged.

The forces in a complex system that resist change are the forces that create the system. In a system that has survived for several generations, the structure has evolved through decades of trial and error. Making a change in one part of the system may have unexpected results in another part of the system or in other systems.

Mapping Resistance to Change

Researchers use two kinds of maps to describe and study the forces within complex systems that resist change. Sometimes, a force is easier to describe with one map than with the other.

Mapping Balancing Feedback

One way of mapping the patterns of complex systems is to picture them as a balancing feedback cycle. A balancing feedback cycle is like a thermostat. If the temperature goes up, the thermostat turns off the furnace. If it goes down, the thermostat turns it on (Senge, 1990).

On this kind of map, complex systems emerge when balancing feedback systems create a stable pattern. If no such feedback patterns exist, there is no system but only disorder. When a change occurs in one part of the system, communication to other parts of the system leads the system to make the necessary adjustments to return the system to normal. As one characteristic increases, it either becomes harder for more of this quality to exist or it becomes easier for a balancing force to develop.

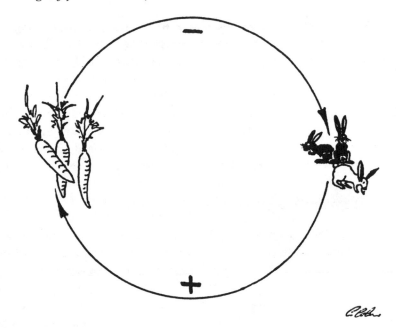

Figure 2.1.

For example, in an ecosystem, if the population of one animal increases, forces soon appear that make it harder on that species. Either the predator population increases or food becomes scarce, so the population levels off (see Figure 2.1).

The human body is an example of a complex adaptive system with millions of kinds of balancing feedback cycles. If the body becomes too hot, sweat glands release moisture. If there is too much sugar in the bloodstream, more insulin is released. If there is too much water, it is eliminated. If a person goes on a diet, metabolism slows down so less food is consumed. If undesirable bacteria enter the body, the immune system eliminates them.

Balancing Feedback in Schools

A balancing feedback map would have predicted what happened at Perryville. As the school changed the way it taught the humanities, parents or the minister noticed a change in the way their young people were thinking and behaving. They responded by attacking CHART to restore the old structure.

Although the most opposition to the CHART project in Perry-ville was from religious groups, in other schools the balancing cycle related to shifts in resources and power. In one school, the band director opposed CHART when it took away his control over the schedule. In another school, opposition mobilized when CHART teachers took desirable space from other uses. Wives, husbands, and children began to complain when CHART activities interfered with summer vacations or evening family activities. Opposition appeared most often when CHART disturbed balances of time and resources.

Attractors and Constraints

Another way of mapping the patterns that keep a complex system stable is adapted from the mathematical concept of attractors (Briggs & Peat, 1989). Picture the choices that individuals make as rain falling on a landscape. Picture the common choices as lakes or rivers that most of the water flows to. Picture the uncommon choices as a small puddle on a mountain peak. Basins of attraction are places that gravity pulls the individual raindrops toward.

Drawing or picturing a landscape of attractors helps us to see what the hard and the easy choices are within our existing system.

For example, the pattern of seats in rows seems to be an attractor state in school structure. Most CHART teaching methods work better with other room arrangements. And in the first year or two of CHART involvement, I would walk into a school and see different room arrangements. But over the years, seats seemed to be guided back into rows by an invisible hand. I have been in classrooms on five continents, with philosophies ranging from Marxist to democratic to tribal preservation, and everywhere I have seen seats in rows.

If we are trying to make a change, a landscape-of-attractors map gives us an idea of how hard that change will be to make and to sustain. If the pattern we are trying to change is at the bottom of a deep basin of attraction, there must be reasons why so many people choose it. If we are trying to change those patterns, we need to know what forces are attracting so many people to make that choice.

The attractors in a landscape can be changed by constructing either dams or pumps. A pump can make water run uphill. A dam can keep it from flowing downhill. If we understand the attractors in our systems, we can reshape our landscapes more effectively—or we can recognize when we are wasting our time.

School Reform Redefined

On a self-organizing systems map, school reform, then, is not a matter of changing programs or of changing structures, it is a process of changing the attractors and constraints or the feedback loops that shape the decisions of the individuals within the system.

These attractors and constraints are not necessarily within the school system. The school, the larger community, and the individual are all part of a complex system of attractors and constraints. The attractors and constraints that affect the school may be in the national budget, or they may be in the religious values in the minds of individuals.

The important question for the survival of reforms is not whether visible projects remain in schools but whether and how the reform has reshaped the landscape of attractors.

Design Limits

According to self-organizing systems theories, a self-organizing system or an individual within a self-organizing system does not have unlimited choices.

Biologist Stuart Kauffman (1993) challenges Darwin's theory that evolution occurs by random mutation. He points out that although an infinite number of mutations may be mathematically possible, the number that are physically and chemically possible is much, much smaller and that each historical choice further limits the range of possibilities.

My experience suggests that there are design limits for schools. I taught at a very innovative school during the 1970s. Faculty worked with the architect to create a unique building architecture as well as imaginative classroom structures. But it was too creative. One year, there was a heavy snowfall, and part of the roof collapsed. The building was beautiful, and I loved its design and its spaces, but the weight of snow made the design unworkable.

Human structures also seemed to have design limits. At Fairview, my colleagues and I tried several new class structures. One, which used an early version of cooperative learning, worked well because it made use of the skills and interests of adolescents. It was built on a landscape in which we manipulated the natural attractors to support us.

Another, a primitive attempt at a writing lab, was a complete failure. My model pushed adolescents to work on things that their natural interests did not draw them to, and I had eliminated the incentives provided by the traditional classroom. Within 2 weeks, the students in my class had subverted my design so they could avoid almost all work.

If we understand the underlying physical, biological, and social landscape on which we are designing our systems, we will have a better chance of avoiding impossible or impractical designs.

What are the attractors and constraints that affect schools? This question needs much more research. The following are areas that I would suggest for exploration.

The Attraction of a Low-Energy Equilibrium State

One attractor state appears to be what chemists call a *low-energy equilibrium system*—the state at which the least expense of energy is necessary. I believe that this defines much of what one sees in school. There seems to be an invisible hand moving toward the system that requires the least expenditure of money and physical and emotional energy. The seats-in-rows classroom model is probably a low-energy equilibrium system. So is textbook-centered and worksheet-centered teaching.

CHART activities tended to be very expensive. Although some of the strategies CHART promoted, such as cooperative learning and portfolio assessment, became efficient and cheap once teachers had the knowledge to implement them, others continued to require a high expenditure of money and energy.

Sometimes, the costs were hidden because they included volunteer time from teachers. One group of CHART teachers estimated that they had averaged 400 unpaid hours of work in the first year of their projects. This time and energy often came from family and leisure time, and teachers were simply not able to sustain this level of dedication for more than 1 or 2 years.

Thelma Tarver, one of the most creative and high-energy teachers I have ever met, developed an exciting program called "Connections" with a team of teachers at Fayetteville, Arkansas, High School. A couple of years after I visited her program, I met her at another meeting and asked how it was going. Sheepishly, she said that they were not doing it. "Connections," she said, "was teaching like I'd always dreamed of teaching. But it was completely exhausting. I simply did not have the energy to sustain it for more than 1 year."

Instinctive and Environmental Behavior Attractors

Research evidence is still quite mixed on the extent to which humans have biologically or genetically programmed default behavior patterns. However, there are patterns of dominance and of nurturance that recur so widely among humans and other species that there must be reasons for their frequency. Irenaus Eibl-Eibesfeldt (1979) provides fascinating drawings of people and animals relating in similar patterns. More recent research suggests a complex interaction between genetic potential and expressed behavior but supports the hypothesis that there are probably genetic patterns that make some kind of behavior more likely than others. In *Emotional Intelligence*, Goleman (1995) presents evidence that early experiences shape a landscape of attractor emotional states.

Cultural and Religious Values

Human beings, unlike other animals or phenomena studied by systems theories, are not limited by low-energy equilibrium states, biological instincts, or environment. We do not always make decisions on the basis of economic benefit. We are, in fact, a species that likes to live on the edge of the impossible, that likes to push ourselves to test our limits.

Cultures and religions create attractors and constraints that lead large numbers of people to choose behaviors that conflict with their natural drives. Moslems fast for a month every year. Christian monks and nuns take vows of chastity. Patriots and religious martyrs defy self-preservation instincts to willingly lay down their lives for a belief. A culture can train children to demand expensive shoes or to wait until after marriage for sexual intercourse. The religious group in Perryville wanted to train children to resist the materialistic values promoted by the media and to make choices based on religious values, regardless of their cost in the modern world.

None of these cultural attractors or constraints control the behavior of everyone in a culture, but they can have a powerful impact on the choices people make.

The religious group in Perryville was correct in recognizing that the CHART project was reshaping young people's values and that this was important.

Knowledge and Skill as Shapers of the Landscape

For teachers, one of the most important shapers of the landscape of attractors is the combination of knowledge and skill. A change in knowledge or skill can change a choice from difficult or even impossible to easy.

Many of the teaching methods that CHART advocated were very difficult to learn; they required that a teacher struggle uphill for several years. However, once mastered, many teachers found methods such as portfolio assessment and cooperative learning were easier than the old methods.

Providing knowledge and skills is one of the most important ways that we can consciously shape our landscape of attractors.

Although the specific program at Perryville did not survive, the ideas it tested and demonstrated are now part of the repertoire of teachers throughout the state. The struggles between the school and community have added to our understanding of the relationship between school and community and religion and school learning. Because we have learned from the experience of Perryville, the capacity of educators around the state is different.

Schools as Shapers of the Attractors
and Constraints of Our Society

Schools are major shapers of the values and behavior patterns that will affect the decisions of the next generation. They provide much of the knowledge base that gives or fails to give the next generation the information it needs to solve problems. The maps of the world and the patterns of thinking that we learned in elementary and high school still affect our thinking, even after we consciously recognize that newer maps are more effective.

The humanities are particularly important in shaping culture. They develop a rich, emotionally laden collection of images, stories, proverbs, and music that guide our preferences and choices. The humanities give a story of our people, their relationships to the natural and supernatural worlds, and our place in that story. They create the image of the group that we are loyal to and evoke the emotions that solidify our loyalty. Music can mobilize our emotions to give us the energy to fight for a cause or to change our way of seeing things. A song or a drumbeat can keep people marching for an ideal or toward a battle long after a rational choice would have been to go home.

Reshaping Both School and Cultural Landscapes

As CHART teachers began to reshape the curriculum to respond to a population of students with African American, Asian American, and Latin American heritage, we suddenly found ourselves the center of controversy. We were caught between Afrocentrists who wanted to reshape the story of history with a center in Africa and whites who feared that admitting multicultural perspectives would weaken the core values that hold our society together.

When we talked about replacing Longfellow with Langston Hughes or Edith Wharton with Toni Morrison, we discovered that people and events that had seemed boring and irrelevant suddenly appeared vitally important. Astounded English and history teachers found themselves the center of heated debates on works that a few years earlier they couldn't bribe students to read. Teachers who were used to hearing that the arts and humanities were frills that were wasting time that should be devoted to science, technology, and business were confronted by parents and politicians who argued that changing a few authors in the literature course and adding multicultural perspectives to history would undermine Western civilization.

As the multicultural debate continued, CHART teachers realized that they were not simply reshaping curriculum but were reshaping the attractors and constraints of our society.

The battle for change in the school is a battle over the shape of our future society. The resistance to change within the school is partly the resistance to change common to self-organizing systems and partly the political resistance to shifts in power within the whole society.

Revising the Goal of School Reform

On a self-organizing systems map, the goal of school reform is not creating and preserving a particular reform but finding and inventing the knowledge and skills necessary for humans to survive in a new era with new challenges. It does not matter whether CHART projects continue to exist. It does not matter whether religious or humanist groups win a particular battle. What does matter is whether we are able to shape cultural attractors that will enable us to survive and thrive in our changing world.

Chapter Three

Mapping Dangers and Opportunities

Although we educators seem to be struggling against the current for every change we want to make, we often find unexpected changes sweeping over us. We struggle for years to develop a program to teach students to use computers, only to discover that suddenly our students can use them better than we can. We spend the summer studying Spanish so we can communicate with our students' parents, only to discover in September that Russian immigrants have moved in while Hispanics have moved out. We plan a unit on the family, only to discover that none of our students are living with a traditional family.

Although our systems are highly resistant to some kinds of change, there is another kind of change that can rapidly transform complex systems. Educators have tended to be victims instead of shapers of this kind of change because it has not been on our maps. These changes tend to happen off the edges of our maps—in other systems that affect schools. And they involve processes that could not be described by our old maps of cause and effect.

Self-organizing system maps make it easier to see the tidal waves coming while we can still protect ourselves and to predict which of our changes are likely to transform systems instead of disappear.

Confronting a Transformational Change

During the spring of 1987, Alberta Arthurs and Judith Rényi came to Arkansas to meet with Governor Bill Clinton about starting a CHART project in Arkansas.

At about the same time, Kenneth "L. A. Moe" Johnson came to town with a quite different vision for the youth of Little Rock. According to a report by the *Arkansas Democrat-Gazette,* Johnson came to Little Rock from Los Angeles in the late 1980s and started the Crips gang (Roth, 1955, p. 1).

In the decade that followed, both the CHART project and the Crips gang spread. However, the spread of the CHART project was slow and painstaking, with every gain the result of a clear expenditure of energy. Gangs seemed to spread as effortlessly and as inexorably as the latest influenza virus. In less than a decade, gangs have had a visible impact on most schools in the metropolitan area that has not only drawn resources away from school services but has directly contradicted the kinds of goals CHART was seeking.

A comparison of the change process stimulated by Johnson and the processes stimulated by CHART illustrates important concepts in the change process.

How Gangs Produced
System Change

Gangs began in a system ripe for change. According to Linda Young (personal communication, June, 1995) of New Futures of Little Rock Youth and the Little Rock School District, gangs are just a symptom of the desperate plight of young people. She says,

> "The real problem is that society has allowed kids to fall into such a state. Undernourished physically, emotionally, and academically, they are susceptible to virus and germs. Kids that have their needs met don't get into these situations. If you meet kids' physical and emotional needs, you will have some slipups but not this wholesale problem. These kids don't feel like they belong anywhere.

Poverty-stricken neighborhoods do not automatically become gang neighborhoods. In the past, many poverty-stricken neighborhoods had organized around churches or extended families to maintain spiritual and personal wealth under conditions of extreme material deprivation.

Creating a Self-Reinforcing Spiral

Gangs created a self-reinforcing spiral in which every step a young person took into the gang destroyed the other choices he or she might have had. Gangs reshaped a child's landscape of attractors to make alternative choices harder and gang choices easier.

Destroying Other Relationships

Gang recruiters build relationships with young people whose ties to family, school, and community are already weak. They offer friendship and support while systematically destroying competing ties with family and nongang friends. For example, a white gang recruiter whom I observed first formed a very close friendship with the other boy, then broke the boy's friendships with others by ridiculing them or by creating situations in which they would be left out or offended. He deliberately created conflicts between the boy, his mother, and his grandparents.

In the meantime, the gang gives the child a sense of belonging, achievement, and power and access to money through selling drugs. Gangs organize criminal activity, set up theft rings, and organize drug businesses. As gang members move up the ranks, they are required to participate in more and more violence. Initiation into a gang may be by being "beaten" in or by committing a crime such as shoplifting. Each move up the ranks usually requires a more serious criminal activity until the highest ranks of gang membership may require murder. One CHART teacher reported that a student told her that he had been ordered to murder her as a gang initiation but had managed to negotiate for another crime instead.

Once a young person has become involved in criminal activity and has a police record, doors are closed to other career choices, activities, and friendships.

Gangs are a serious and lucrative business. The drug trade has transferred money from adults to street toughs. Gang members can make up to $500 on a good day in the drug trade. Teenage gang members making this kind of money, in a community in which working adults were barely surviving on minimum wage, gained unhealthy amounts of power. The drug trade, of course, further weakens the community and leads to further neglect of children, leading to a new generation of potential gang members. Drug money also allows gang members to arm themselves heavily, which starts a spiral of violence.

Violence becomes an addiction. There is a thrill in living on the edge of violence. There is a kind of power. Violence also progressively cuts off human feelings and the ability to build other kinds of relationships. In gang culture, an insult must be avenged. A gang member who has committed an act of violence against another gang must constantly watch his back and be prepared to strike preemptively.

So the gang sets up a powerful spiral of violence. The more involved the child becomes with the gang, the easier it is to continue and the harder it becomes to leave. As gangs spread, they weaken community forces, making more children vulnerable. As gangs gain power through violence, others resort to violence either in defense or because they see the gang as the center of power. Young people caught in a gang-controlled neighborhood see joining the gang as the only form of protection.

Reaching the Limits to Growth

For awhile, it looked as if gangs would expand indefinitely. However, their growth seemed to reach limits. The crime rate in Little Rock reached a peak in 1993. As would be expected in a complex system threatened by change, society acted vigorously to limit and eliminate the threat. Society rushed to fill the cracks in its attractors and reinforced the limiting cycles. The police force was expanded and changed its strategies, and new youth programs were designed to provide young people with attractive alternatives to gangs. Parents and young people were warned of the dangers and were trained to resist.

Gang members themselves began to realize that the results of their efforts had been the opposite of what they had intended. They had expected to become wealthy from dealing in drugs, but instead, they found themselves trapped in burned-out and boarded-up neighborhoods. They had expected to gain power, but instead of attacking the power structure, they found themselves killing each other. Between 1990 and 1992, Arkansas's homicide rate for black males aged 15 to 19 doubled, and by 1993, homicide was the state's leading cause of death for nonwhite males and females between 15 and 24 years old (Roth, 1995).

By 1995, Moe Johnson himself was trying to stop the bandwagon that he had helped start. Serving a 15-year prison term for aggravated assault, gun, theft, and drug charges, he had time to worry about the world young gang members were creating for themselves. The young men he had recruited were killing each other at an alarming rate in neighborhoods that were even more poverty-stricken and devastated than before. Moe Johnson joined with leaders of rival gangs who were in the same prison to make an appeal on closed-circuit television to the young people left on the streets to stop fighting and go back to school.

Between 1993 and 1996, aggravated assaults dropped from 4,468 in 1993 to 1,725 in 1996 (Kordsmeier, 1997). Most indicators suggest that gangs have reached their peak in Little Rock and that gang activity has leveled off and dropped. However, society has not exactly returned to its original shape. Neighborhoods that once had small and old but peaceful homes now have burned-out shells, boarded-up houses, or houses with iron bars on doors and windows. Schools now have metal detectors and police officers. The resources that once went to curriculum development are now devoted to security.

The Mechanisms of Change

The rapid growth of gangs illustrates *snowballing,* one of the processes by which self-organizing systems change. The process of snowballing has been independently discovered in a number of fields and has been given a number of names, such as *bandwagon effect, positive feedback cycle, autocatalysis, reinforcing processes,* or *escalating processes.* All of these labels describe a process in which the more you have of something, the more you get.

I will use the term *snowballing* to refer to this process because it is widely used in both the popular and the technical literature. The larger a snowball is, the more snow that will stick to it.

"Getting on the bandwagon" is another way the process is described in popular language. In many human activities, the more people who do something, the more others are attracted to it. If the bandwagon is about a product, the more products are sold and typically, the more cheaply they can be made so yet more people are attracted to them.

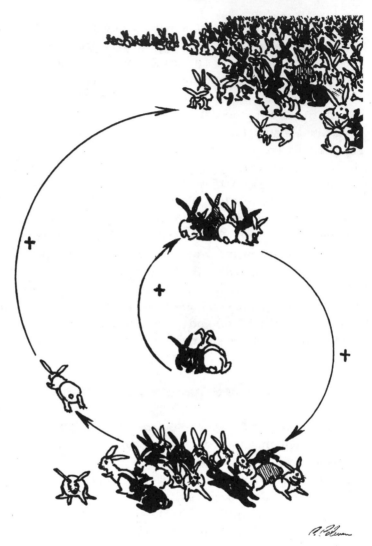

Figure 3.1.

Positive feedback cycle is a technical term that describes the way such a cycle is shown on a systems diagram (see Figure 3.1). As one part of a cycle increases, the other side also increases.

Chemists use the term *autocatalysis* to describe a reaction in which a chemical reaction produces a substance that then makes the reaction happen faster.

Peter M. Senge (1990), in *The Fifth Dimension,* describes the process of making small changes from reinforcing feedback: "In reinforcing processes . . . a small change builds on itself. Whatever movement occurs is amplified, producing more movement in the same direction. A small action snowballs with more and more and still more of the same, resembling compounding interest" (p. 81).

A snowballing or bandwagon process rapidly reshapes the landscape of attractors. The more people who make the choice, the more attractive the choice becomes. For example, the first person who drives over a snowy road has many equal choices. However, the second person on the road finds it easier to follow the tracks of the first car. Soon, the ruts may be so deep that it is very difficult for a driver to make a different choice.

Snowballing as the Engine of Change

Snowballing processes are the engines of change in self-organizing systems. As we have seen in previous chapters, self-organizing systems are extremely resistant to change under fairly constant conditions, but they are capable of dramatic change and reorganization when change becomes necessary for survival. The whole system may be completely reorganized with a new landscape of attractors in a phase transition. According to Senge (1990), "Whenever you are in a situation where things are growing, you can be sure that reinforcing feedback is at work" (p. 71).

Experimentation

According to Prigogine's research, the changes in a self-organizing system begin when the system becomes disrupted by fluctuations or changes in the outside environment that are too great for it to absorb. At this point, there are wild fluctuations as the system "experiments" with a range of different behaviors. The attractors collapse, and the system "explores" a wide range of possibilities. The system may go in several directions. The fluctuations may continue indefinitely, the system may use limiting cycles to stop change, the system may collapse, or one of the changes may trigger a process of autocatalysis. At some point, one of the choices may begin a process of autocatalysis that quickly reorganizes the system into a new pattern.

As the new process spreads rapidly, it makes alternatives less possible and sets up a new regime of attractors (Prigogine & Stengers, 1984).

As we saw in the Perryville example in the last chapter, different individuals or groups will perceive the problem differently and will develop different solutions.

Competition

As a variety of new structures is invented, intense competition among inventions may develop. We saw such a competition in Perryville. Unfortunately, in complex systems, the competition is not necessarily won by the best idea nor by the most politically astute group. The process of reorganization is unpredictable and does not give the advantage to the good or the beautiful or even necessarily the fittest. The advantage goes to the competitor who can set up the most powerful self-reinforcing spiral. Gangs had absolutely nothing to offer the system. However, they set up a powerful autocatalytic process and restructured our neighborhoods and our schools.

Self-organizing systems do not change to a new form because the new form is better but because a positive feedback system is set up that changes the attractor system.

Lock-In

According to Waldrop (1992), economist Brian Arthur used the term *lock-in* to describe the way a snowballing change eliminates alternative solutions and sets up a new set of attractors in a system. He challenged the concept of traditional economics that the most efficient change would win in competition and demonstrated that snowballing changes could eliminate more efficient solutions that did not snowball.

He illustrated the concept with the QWERTY typewriter keyboard. It was actually designed to slow down typists in the days when typewriters jammed easily. However, the more typewriters that were built with this keyboard, the more typists learned it and demanded that new typewriters have this keyboard. Today, no one would buy a keyboard laid out alphabetically. The self-reinforcing cycle created a new attractor state and locked in a new, but inferior, pattern. The system settles into a new attractor state and again resists change (Waldrop, 1992).

Snowballing processes never continue indefinitely. Balancing processes may level them out and return the system to its original shape, as happened in CHART's rural showcase school. Or the system may incorporate a small change as happened with gang culture. Occasionally, however, the change leads to a complete system re-organization. If, for example, home schooling or privitization create a powerful enough snowball effect, they could lock in a completely different system of education in the United States. Philip Schlechty (1997) warns that the move to private schools could lock out a public school system while not solving the problems it is designed to solve.

> Unfortunately, by the time it becomes clear that the problems are systems problems, rather than a public school-private school issue, the dismantling of our educational systems will be so far along that, like Humpty Dumpty, the system will not be capable of being put back together again. (p. 20)

Per Bak (1996) hypothesizes that on the edge of chaos, one cannot predict which changes will be absorbed by the system and which will lead to a complete restructuring. He says that a system on the edge of chaos is like a pile of sand with grains of sand dropped on it. Most grains will create very small disruptions, but occasionally, one grain will create an avalanche that will change the shape of a whole pile.

Schools today probably are on the edge of chaos. As Prigogine predicted, they are full of contradictory experiments seeking new solutions. So far, none of the potential changes has created an uncontrollable snowball and locked in a new system. However, such a change seems quite probable in the near future.

Making Innovations Snowball

So far, educators have done very little to make their own desired processes snowball. Snowballing is a process that we cannot completely control, but we may be able to influence it much more than we have.

The role of snowballing was generally missing in the mental maps of school reformers or researchers until it was described in Peter Senge's (1990) *The Fifth Discipline*. I do not recall hearing any discussion of snowballing or positive feedback spirals except in reference to the curriculum-assessment loop in any CHART discussions. The role of snowballing in systems change has received very little comment in the literature on educational change. It still is inadequately considered in planning school reforms, and I suspect that the absence of this concept has played an important role in our failure to understand or manage change effectively.

In CHART, we rarely asked questions about snowballing, such as, "Will this change affect the landscape of attractors? Will my doing this change make it easier and more likely for others to do it, and will it make it easier for me to repeat it?"

If we had asked these questions, we would have made many different decisions in CHART. For example, giving teachers small minigrants made it much more likely that they would implement changes in their courses. However, the minigrants almost guaranteed that they would create the kind of changes that would not snowball. A teacher would not have a minigrant the next year, and the teachers around them did not have minigrants, so the grant-dependent reform would die. Without the minigrants, we probably would have had fewer initial results, but we might have had more inventions that snowballed.

Reforms that depended on increasing teachers' knowledge were more likely to snowball. The teacher's knowledge increases while he or she uses the innovation—it becomes easier with practice, and the teacher's knowledge can be shared with other teachers.

Portfolio or authentic assessment sometimes set up a snowball effect and changed the landscape of attractors. With assessment tools that required students to write essays or solve complex problems, teachers had to change the way they taught to avoid failure. And once they had changed their curricula, it was easier to continue than to go back to the old ways. But it took a long time and a lot of investment before the new ways became easier. In most schools, it seemed to take about 5 years of heavy investment of energy, time, and resources to learn the new ways and develop the resource base to support them.

It is as if you have to spend a lot of time going uphill before you can cross the barriers to set up a new regime of attractors. Many changes do not snowball on a small scale. It takes a critical mass to start the snowballing process.

Our old maps led us to value the wrong changes. We assumed that the more changes you had the first year, the more you were likely to have the second year. The new maps tell us that one strong snowball is worth thousands of changes that do not change the landscape of attractors.

Learning to Manage Unwanted Snowballs

Recognizing Snowballs

Educators need to be alert for snowballing processes that will affect schools. Snowballing processes start small. Many of them can be stopped or changed if they are detected early, but because they are small and people do not understand the process of snowballing, they usually ignore the signs. For example, once Little Rock recognized and faced the problems of gangs, a number of smaller communities in Arkansas recognized that gangs were trying to spread to their communities. They were able to stop the spread much earlier.

Snowballing processes that affect schools may be located in different systems. Today, major avalanches from outside the schools threaten to engulf the entire educational system. Technology is rapidly changing the relationship between human beings, information, and learning. Social, economic, and demographic changes are undermining support for the public schools.

Technology is probably the most powerful creator of snowballing cycles in human history. Television has already restructured the way young people use their time and the way their minds develop. Television not only takes time away from reading but seems to shape minds to lack the imagination to bring alive details from print and to want constant change and stimulation. So reading becomes even less attractive.

As computers become more widely available and as educational software becomes more powerful, the most attractive way of teaching different topics changes, and the method of teaching changes what we learn. Already, there are major changes in the way mathematics is taught and thought about. The next generation will have quite different mathematical skills and capabilities than our generation. They will have much less computational skill—and will therefore be even more dependent on electronic devices. If the results of current teaching are as intended, they will be much more skillful at using mathematics to solve complex problems with many variables. They may therefore use computers to solve problems that we would have used our intuition to solve. They will therefore be even more dependent on computers and more likely to map their world with mathematics.

Mehlinger (1996) writes,

> The forces driving the Information Age seem irresistible. It is impossible both to participate fully in the culture and yet resist its defining features. . . . It [Information Age technology] is changing the landscape of American culture in ways we either take for granted or scarcely notice. (p. 402)

Managing Snowballs

We usually cannot stop powerful snowballs, but we may be able to shape their paths. The most effective response to snowballs may be to tame and harness them. Societies that have survived have managed the use of technology for their benefit and have set up rules and taboos to stop harmful uses. One of the earliest and still most dangerous technologies was fire. Societies that survived learned to control fire. We do not know how many were destroyed by misuse of fire. Even today, after thousands of years of successful use of fire by our ancestors, each of us individually has to be taught fire safety, and we still have to have a legal system to control arsonists.

Human history does not provide many examples of societies that were successful in deliberately resisting technological inventions. Chinese emperors were among the most successful historical figures at controlling the choices of technology that their people were allowed to use. However, the long-term result was that the Chinese were unable to compete with the Europeans who took Chinese inventions, such as gunpowder, and developed them further. Religious values have enabled some groups, such as the Amish, to maintain a lifestyle that avoids contemporary technology. But such groups remain small.

One of the primary functions of culture is to manage self-reinforcing spirals. Most cultures set up constraints to manage addicting substances and potentially addicting behaviors. By providing information about long-term effects and by providing powerful emotional and social constraints, they encourage people to avoid the most obvious addiction spirals.

Self-reinforcing spirals are often so large that they are not visible in the individual lifetime or experience. They delude people because their initial results appear good. One of the important functions of history and literature is to make visible the long-term results of short-term choices.

At a time of rapid change, we need to draw on the broadest range of cultural resources to help us develop patterns for managing and shaping our snowballing world.

Part Two

Using Your New Maps to Guide the Change Process

How do you start on the road to change? In the first section of this book, you learned some new ways to map the change process. This section will give you some guided tours through various parts of the change process. The chapters in this section will guide you through new approaches to developing a vision, building a knowledge base, finding allies, managing conflict, and monitoring your results. In each chapter, you will have examples of CHART educators' uses of the new maps and some suggestions to help you use them. In some chapters, you will find new concepts to add to your maps. The last chapter suggests ways of remapping your own personal relationship to and attitude toward change.

Chapter Four

Developing a Vision in a World You Don't Own

At a recent workshop, two teachers argued over where the change process starts. "It starts with a vision or a dream," said the first teacher.

"No, it starts with a picture of reality and an awareness of need," the second argued. "The dream grows out of the awareness of need."

It is a subtle difference but an important one. The old mechanical maps showed the change agent as a builder planning and making a machine. On the new maps, we are part of the systems we are changing. We are only one of many stockholders. We found that recognizing our position in a larger system made a big difference in our dreams and in the chances our dreams had of succeeding.

Problems With the Old Maps

When Arkansas joined the CHART network, we started our first workshop by using the traditional mental maps and tools of the 1980s. To join the project, each school team of four teachers had written a proposal stating a rationale and specific objectives for their project. We began by having each school team present its goals and objectives on newsprint, which was hung on the walls. It was all very boring and unreal. Each team dutifully presented a nice map of the future with a broad goal and a set of specific objectives (some of them stated in behavioral terms), and we all tried to stifle the yawns. There was a lot of jargon about multicultural, restructuring, and interdisciplinary, a lot of vague platitudes about commitment to all students, but there was not a lot of enthusiasm or a very clear sense of reality.

The objectives sounded very familiar. They were the objectives we all knew we were supposed to have, not the values we really cared about. We'd all been down this same road for decades, and none of us liked where we'd gotten to.

Developing a Humanities Approach to Vision Building

It was time for a humanities break. We pulled out a collection of masks from other countries and talked about the mythical journey of the hero through masks that hid deeper truths and monsters that challenged the path. Then, we gave the teams butcher paper and magic markers, with instructions to draw the journey the team was hoping to take from the school of the present to the school of their dreams and the monsters they expected to meet on the way.

With images of colorful, frightening, and humorous masks in their minds and crayons in their hands, the teams got down to business. When they gathered to share dreams, there were no more plastic objectives and no more straight-line journeys. There were pictures of racism, isolation, poverty, and fear. There were images of frightened, isolated schools trying to wall out the electronic, multicultural, international world that was engulfing them and their beloved forests and mountains. There were pictures of dragons and monsters on the route to change. There were a lot of smiles and laughter, which made it possible for people to say the things they usually hid behind masks.

John said,

This is our school today. It is a building without any windows. Outside is a world that is changing rapidly, but nobody wants to see it. My students want to stay hidden in our piney woods, but our timber is being cut and shipped to Japan. Their parents' jobs depend on an international economy, but they are afraid to think of any place outside the county. I want to open up windows on the world.

The team from another rural school shared John's sense of isolation. "Send us a real, live person from another country because my kids don't even believe they exist," begged Bettina, only half joking. But isolation was not her school's biggest problem. The two races in the town still lived in a prison of racism.

Said Willifene,

> What we really want is for the white leaders who still control this community and who send their children to private schools to recognize that we exist and to see the good things we're doing in the school and to see that all these little black kids in the school aren't dumb and lazy.

"I just have this hunch," she went on, "that if we had more contact with people from outside, even from other countries, we'd be able to understand each other better."

Jerome, Dorothy, and Beth worried that race relations were deteriorating among their students or that a surface politeness was giving way to active hostility. Jerome shared his dream of turning the school. Dorothy and Beth were skeptical, but Jerome argued that because old ideas weren't working, it might be the time for a bold new plan.

The visions that came out of the second session expressed the teachers' deepest fears, frustrations, dreams, and values. At the planning sessions that followed, teachers developed strategies for reaching their dreams with their unique students and for circumventing their local dragons. They came up with plans that they cared about and were committed to.

The visions that guided real change were based on each individual sharing experiences of reality. They were based on different perceptions of the needs both of the schools and of the larger society. Although the visions had much in common, there was no consensus and no attempt to build consensus. In a self-organizing system, both structure and change come from the interaction of individual choices, not from a single, coordinated vision.

Furthermore, the vision was constantly evolving as we reflected both on the deep values of our culture and on the results of our actions.

Vision Evolved From Reflecting on the Deep Values of Our Heritage

Because CHART was a humanities project, we spent a lot of time reflecting on our heritage as human beings, Americans, teachers, and members of specific ethnic or regional groups. These experiences created a depth to our vision. Most of the strategies that we developed can be used by any kind of change group.

One of our favorite activities for beginning work with a group was to ask everyone to bring a poem, song, story, picture, or object that had been important in developing their core values. This activity allowed people to share religious experiences, ethnic or family heritage, or personal tragedies that school settings did not usually allow to be discussed. The sharing usually led to a deep understanding of both common values and experiences and respect for differences.

We did not attempt to reach any kind of consensus on core values. In Arkansas, many of our teachers were deeply religious, from faiths with contradictory beliefs. A Baptist, an atheist, a Catholic, and a sort-of-Buddhist could not reach consensus on their beliefs, but they could respond to each others' music or poetry and the life experiences that made those works meaningful.

In many of the CHART projects, the teachers, project staff, humanities consultants, students, and community members spent several years exploring and refining their understanding of the deep values of their heritage. Our vision of our heritage became deeper and broader as we wrestled with the texts and artifacts that showed our ancestors' conflicts, values, and decisions. In a time of rapid change, it became particularly important to find ourselves in a longer, larger story.

This quest for a new vision, of course, was not a matter of a few days' workshop. Bonnie Davis (1994) described the way her vision of her place in a multicultural society grew over years of participating in CHART workshops. Bonnie, a teacher in the St. Louis, Missouri, area, began attending workshops on African American literature at the International Education Consortium to help connect a growing population of African American students who were being bussed into her schools. Her vision, however, grew from reading a few books to a major scholarly interest (p. 221).

She joined a study tour to Senegal, West Africa, with other CHART teachers. During the next year, she introduced African literature to her classes and met regularly with other teachers who were using the same works. From the discussion of African literature, students moved into a discussion of language, noting that most modern African writers write in French and English. The African American students began to express frustration at the way teachers reacted to their dialect, so the faculty invited an expert in Black English to do an inservice workshop for them.

Students were so inspired by the program that they formed a multicultural club, which visited ethnic restaurants and attended lectures presented by the local World Affairs Council. They became involved in United Nations simulations and attended films on apartheid and raised money for a Red Cross center in Senegal. They got involved in race relations forums and participated in a live television show on diversity.

As Ms. Davis (1994) put it, "What began as a means to create connections for students evolved into a way of life" (p. 228).

Vision Evolved From Reflection on Practice

Exploring and reflecting on literature and the arts expanded our sense of what is important and what creates enduring value, but we found that teachers also needed a concrete image of classroom practices and school structures. The kind of teaching that we were trying to promote did not have a simple road map. Teachers did not start each class with a set plan and objectives. Instead, the lesson emerged out of the interaction of the students, the teacher, and the text.

Dr. Judith Rényi, the director of CHART, used several strategies to build a common vision of quality humanities teaching. She organized national conferences at which the best teachers from around the country presented demonstration lessons, which were critiqued and discussed. At one of the project directors' meetings, she asked the directors to write a description of a lesson they had seen that represented high-quality humanities teaching. At another meeting, she invited a group of scholars who had done research on defining quality in the social studies. The task of reaching consensus was much harder than we had anticipated. We all knew that we wanted students to think, to understand issues in depth, and to be actively involved in learning, but each of those concepts can be interpreted in a number of ways. We never reached a consensus definition of quality in the humanities, but each of us individually developed a much deeper ability to perceive quality and weaknesses.

Although most CHART project directors preferred developing a vision from the participants and refining it through dialogue and assessment, many of our funders wanted us to state a vision in clearly defined principles or goals that could be evaluated. Several other school reform projects, such as the Coalition of Essential Schools and the Goodlad network, seemed to be having a lot of success by organizing around a set of common principles, and we were encouraged to use the same approach. We did make an attempt and developed six common principles, but we continued to argue over whether stating principles improved the project.

Whereas we saw a number of schools that successfully reorganized around a predetermined model or set of principles, we also saw many examples of a focus on abstract principles leading to poor thinking.

First, when a set of common principles or a change model was presented by a fund or an administrator, the discussion frequently deteriorated into groupthink. Anyone who raised questions not only risked being labeled as a troublemaker or resistant to change by the administrator but faced heavy peer pressure from colleagues who wanted the grant or the administrator's approval or who supported the principles.

Second, a focus on abstract principles focused attention away from the real world conditions that need to be considered in a complex, rapidly changing world. After one CHART workshop that had included a list of CHART goals that included interdisciplinary teaching, one team met me almost in tears. "We feel like a failure," they said. "We haven't been able to get an interdisciplinary program going."

"Do you think you could teach more effectively if you had an interdisciplinary program?" I asked.

"Not really," they admitted.

Our courses just don't fit together the way they do in the states that have developed the model programs. In fact, we haven't thought of any significant themes in which our disciplines over-lap. But we want to be a good CHART project so we want to be interdisciplinary.

Whereas no approach to vision setting worked perfectly, the approach of sharing dreams and problems through the arts and then continuing to evaluate and reflect on the results seemed a much more powerful planning process than setting abstract goals and principles or objectives.

When teachers reflected on concrete examples instead of abstract principles, they were better able to see the unique characteristics of the classroom and to select those that best fit their situations. Humanities approaches also mobilized their feelings and emotions as well as their rational processes.

Understanding Vision in Complex Adaptive Systems

Complex system maps explain why a humanities approach to decision making is more appropriate to a rapidly changing complex system than traditional goal- or principle-based models. Complex systems on the edge of chaos have two characteristics that affect the way we set visions: interdependence and adaptability.

Interdependence

The school, like other complex systems, is a system within systems within systems.

Many of the vision-setting ideas now used in schools have been adapted from corporate change strategies, but corporations are a different type of system. Corporation managers can develop a vision or a set of principles because they own the corporations or are hired by the owners. If their visions don't fit the needs of the world, their corporation goes bankrupt or they lose their jobs.

A school faculty does not own the school or the children who come to it. Teachers and administrators are part of a community. The purpose of schooling is often defined as the transmission of culture. The culture is not something that teachers own. Schools are in both a weaker and a stronger position than corporations in vision setting.

They are weaker because they cannot set a vision that is independent of the community and the national culture. On the other hand, they have a powerful impact on the national and community culture because they do influence the enculturation of the next generation. The vision of a school needs both to reflect and shape the vision of society as a whole.

In systems terminology, schools are open or interdependent, adaptive systems. On a systems map, a school would be seen as a part of or related to a number of other systems—families, the community, the state, and the nation. The school cannot set an independent course or develop an independent vision. The state, the community, and the nation already have visions for the school. A school faculty's vision is a part of the overall community vision, not independent from it.

A story told by a Benedictine nun illustrates the difference between an independent vision and a vision rooted in the real world:

> A teacher once told his students that it is easier to travel than to stop.
>
> The students asked why.
>
> The teacher replied that "As long as you travel to a goal, you can hold on to a dream. When you stop, you must face reality."
>
> "But how shall we ever change if we have no goals or dreams?" the disciples asked.
>
> "Change that is real is change that is not willed. Face reality and unwilled change will happen." (Chittister, 1990, p. 53)

Adaptation Versus Reshaping

Peter Senge and several other current writers on school change talk about the need to turn the school into learning organizations, which he defines as "organizations where people continually expand their capacity to create the results they truly desire, where new and expansive patterns of thinking are nurtured, where collective aspiration is set free, and where people are continually learning how to learn together" (Senge, 1990, p. 3).

The Santa Fe group of researchers use the term *complex adaptive systems* and presents a slightly different picture of an organization's learning and potential. Murray Gell-Mann, who won the Nobel prize for discovering the quark, explains, "Complex adaptive [systems]

. . . interact with the environment, 'learn' from the experience, and adapt as a result" (as quoted in Lewin, 1992, p. 15).

In the complex adaptive systems model developed by Gell-Mann and his colleagues at the Santa Fe Institute, the world is filled with systems within systems within systems, constantly changing, adapting, and learning in response to both external and internal changes. In this vision, schools are already complex adaptive systems, and they continually evolve in response to environmental change.

In other words, schools already are learning organizations. They have evolved to their present structures by learning and adapting to previous conditions. Brouillette (1996), in *A Geology of School Reform*, documents the way three generations of school reform in a district were instituted in response to different times and how the previous learning of the institution affects its current capacity. She emphasizes that present decisions about change are deeply affected by the way the school or the school district adapted to previous conditions and that people are more responsive to new changes if their previous contributions are acknowledged.

The Santa Fe model, although it emphasizes the history of change, tends to overemphasize adaptation because it is based primarily on studies of nonhuman systems. Senge (1990) emphasizes humans' capacity for reshaping the environment. Senge points out that "for a learning organization, 'adaptive learning' must be joined by 'generative learning,' learning that enhances our capacity to create" (p. 14). Human systems, unlike the physical, chemical, computer, and biological systems that many of Gell-Mann's colleagues study, can be guided by conscious goals.

On a self-organizing system map, vision is not a single idea that all members of the group adhere to, but it is an evolving deliberation of different perceptions of needs and dreams.

Some Suggestions for Developing Vision and Goals in a Complex System

Step 1. Develop Roots and Connections to Your Community and Your Culture.

A good way to begin a change process is to review your school's history and to celebrate and acknowledge the people who met past challenges.

It is important to set a vision for a new change within a long historic context of the dreams and struggles of a people and within the short historical context of the local school. The people who set up and maintain the system you want to change are more likely to be supportive if you recognize and appreciate their history and acknowledge the extent to which the systems and programs they developed were wise responses to previous situations and if you treat their work with respect. The present system is there because it "learned" previous lessons. Acknowledgment of existing values makes people more ready to participate in change.

Step 2. Use the Arts to Share Multiple Perspectives on Your Current Reality.

Once a group has become aware of and acknowledged its history, it needs to name and define its present reality. An artistic representation, such as a drawing or a role play, usually helps a group be more honest and open about troubling and controversial issues. Paolo Freire (as paraphrased in Wallenstein, 1987) called this technique *coding*—creating a concrete representation of an issue that "represents the group's reality" and "allows them to project their emotional and social responses in a focused fashion." A code allows a group to deal with "loaded issues that may be too threatening to approach directly or too overwhelming or embarrassing to confront individually" (p. 39).

I liked to use a description of a school or classroom situation by a skilled writer such as John Holt or a collection of photographs that focused on changes in society.

Begin the discussion by asking different participants to tell what they see in the text or pictures and how it relates to their own experiences. As a picture of the school or the changing world emerges, move to a discussion of the ways they would like to see change. Share the visions, but respect different perspectives.

Step 3. Set Modest Goals and Adjust Them as Needed.

In a complex system, modest visions and goals tend to be more useful than more grandiose and universal visions. In a self-organizing system, you have a limited influence over a limited number of the decisions that shape the system. It is fantasy and usually counterproductive to develop a vision that is larger than your sphere of influence.

Instead of reaching a common definition of an issue, it may be more productive to reach a common recognition of the range of perspectives. Instead of reaching agreement on a common set of principles for restructuring schools, it may be more useful to agree to try grade level teams for a year and evaluate their impacts. In general, your goals should encompass what the people in the room can achieve in the time frame that they are willing to commit to. However, your vision needs to include the way that your goals and actions connect to those of the other people in your school and your community.

Provide ongoing opportunities for people to reflect and develop the next steps in the vision. Michael Fullan (1993), in *Change Forces*, says that a vision needs to evolve from action. "Trying to get everyone on board in advance of action cannot work because it does not connect to the reality of dynamic complexity. . . . Deep ownership comes through learning that arises from full engagement in solving problems" (p. 31).

Step 4: Reflect on Your Results and Revise Your Vision or Set New Goals.

Periodically, gather as much information as possible about your progress, and reflect on your results. In CHART, we brought teachers together four times a year to reflect on their evolving projects and their changing visions. If your project has generated opposition, invite your opponents to share in your evaluation process if they are reasonable people who share your basic concern for students but disagree on specifics. Let your vision evolve from your experience and reflection on the experience.

Chapter Five

Building a Knowledge Base for Change

As you develop a vision for change, you probably recognize that you need new skills or knowledge. How do you know what knowledge you need to implement your new vision? How do you learn the new skills?

To make complex changes in complex systems, we need much more knowledge and a more sophisticated way of mapping our knowledge needs.

Linda Darling-Hammond (1995) writes that previous efforts at school reform "were undermined . . . by underinvestment in teachers and in school capacity" (p. 36).

Both traditional mechanical maps and complex system maps show knowledge as needed for change. The difference between traditional maps and self-organizing systems maps is in the way they map knowledge. In a self-organizing system, each individual must have enough knowledge to make wise decisions.

Problems With Traditional Maps of Knowledge

Our traditional maps pictured knowledge as something that was measurable and countable. When we looked for knowledge using those maps, we saw the parts of it that are measurable and countable. The kinds of knowledge that are most measurable and countable are procedures and facts.

Procedures and facts are easy to teach and easy to assess. Staff development workshops of the 1980s typically focused on a set of procedures. CHART workshops initially presented new content. Neither kind of workshop provided all of the knowledge that was needed.

More complex structures, almost by definition, require greater knowledge. Most school reformers, in my experience, vastly underestimate the amount of new knowledge that their reform requires because they map only procedures and factual content. Maps looking for measurable, countable knowledge omitted much of the important knowledge.

Mapping the Knowledge Needed for Change

CHART teachers went through workshops both on methods and procedures and methods on content. The best teachers were able to take what they learned in a workshop and combine it with their vast store of other kinds of knowledge and use the new methods. I wondered why all teachers were not able to use our content and procedures effectively. Finally, I realized that they were missing the knowledge that had been invisible on our old maps.

Mapping the Knowledge Needed for Cooperative Learning

Many of our CHART teachers went through a weeklong workshop on cooperative learning. Many tried to implement the new concepts as they revised their curriculum. But the results from different teachers were quite different.

I visited two schools to observe social studies teachers doing cooperative learning. At the first school, the students did a very brief, not very successful, group activity. The teacher said, "I went through a whole week of training and I did everything they said, but it really didn't work very well." My observation confirmed her impression. She had, indeed, followed the procedures, and she was correct that they had not worked very well.

The second teacher had attended a similar workshop several years earlier and had been using the method regularly. Her students quickly organized themselves into groups and began to undertake complex, sophisticated tasks with little supervision. I spent 4 hours taking notes from the teacher and was astounded by the depth of her knowledge. She not only knew, applied, and refined every concept from the weeklong workshop, but she had expanded that knowledge through trial and error. She could have run a 4-week workshop on the procedures of cooperative learning. It had taken her years of practice to reach this level of expertise.

But she not only knew cooperative learning procedures; she also had a deep knowledge of the psychology and sociology of her classes. She knew each student's learning style. She knew the students' families and what kind of support or problems she could expect from them. She knew what help the resource teacher could offer and how to structure a class so the resource teacher could be effective. She had a close relationship with the librarian and not only knew what resources the librarian could provide but also how to get the librarian to provide her many more resources than she routinely provided.

Furthermore, she had a much deeper knowledge of her subject matter than the first teacher. The teacher who found cooperative learning unsuccessful stuck very close to the textbook. When students asked questions that went beyond the textbook, she was lost and uncomfortable. Her ideas about how to organize the knowledge that she had were limited. She only knew how to think of history chronologically.

The teacher who used cooperative learning effectively had a detailed mental map of the textbook, but she had a whole bookshelf worth of additional knowledge in her head. She was able to manipulate and reorganize her knowledge in a variety of ways. She could see connections between history and science. She could trace historical trends backwards from the present, or she could trace inventions across cultures, or she could examine themes and issues without reference to chronology. As a result, the tasks, materials, and assignments she gave her students were much more interesting and challenging and connected to the students' natural interests.

Mapping the Knowledge Needed for New Content

CHART leaders recognized the limits of so-called process workshops, but we discovered that traditional content workshops were not sufficient either. We started out with a high estimate of the amount of knowledge our reforms would need. CHART director Judith Rényi once said that she expected the CHART collaborative to invest about $10,000 over a 3-year period in education for each participating teacher. That was a good estimate for teachers who came to us with strong background knowledge in their subjects and good knowledge of their students. But teachers with weak backgrounds were still far from the goal even after 3 years.

The first CHART project in Philadelphia took a single course from the curriculum and tried to move beyond the textbook maps. Rényi, who began her career with CHART as director of this project, recalled that it grew out of almost unanimous agreement by social studies teachers that the world history course was a disaster. It was totally European history and did not have a clear place for the United States or for the 60% of the kids in the class who were not of European ancestry.

The teachers recognized that the textbook map of world history left out much that was important to them. They saw their goal as filling in the gaps. They wanted a new textbook that filled in the gaps and some workshops that would fill in their own gaps in knowledge.

But Rényi (as quoted in Beard, 1992) believed that the problem was deeper than the specific gaps in a specific textbook. She believed that the very concept of a textbook created a bad model of history. She said,

> Textbooks give a very wrong message, I think, especially about history, but probably about most disciplines, that "within this bound volume, truth lies." The whole purpose of this curriculum is to say, that's not true. You, the student, create truth and you evaluate that truth. You have to evaluate data and you have to evaluate the sources that that comes from, and we're teaching you some interpretations that scholars have found valid and valuable, but you're creating truth out of this. The [CHART] curriculum says an important thing because it changes. Every time it comes out, once a year, it's different, and it will always be. (p. 270)

The Philadelphia project pioneered the CHART emphasis on dealing with knowledge in more complex ways. Rényi sometimes described the new goal as "thinking like a historian." She wanted students to examine evidence, make hypotheses, and make critical judgments about new information instead of simply adding the bits of new information together. History was not just a collection of facts but a pattern of organizing mental processes to interpret those facts.

The Philadelphia curriculum development project built teams of teachers and scholars to work on units of the new curriculum. The process of developing each unit began with a seminar presented by scholars to the teachers and was followed by the teachers and scholars working together. The scholars indicated resources or significant episodes that the teachers ought to look at and modeled new teaching approaches. The teachers took the material from the scholars and put it into teaching units, which they then took back to the scholars to evaluate (Beard, 1992, p. 263).

The curriculum was difficult to produce, but it was even more difficult to implement. Most of the teachers had been trained in the era when knowledge had been mapped and stored in textbooks by curriculum specialists. A curriculum-writing team or textbook authors had the knowledge of the content and made all of the decisions and mapped every step of the journey. They produced materials that were simple enough to teach so that a person with little knowledge or sophistication could lead students through it. I remember being told, as a textbook author in the 1970s, that I should assume that the teacher knew nothing about the subject and should design a teacher's guide that included all of the information, all of the questions, and all of the answers that a teacher would need to teach the lessons.

The result of decades of relying on "teacher-proof" textbooks was that teachers' internal maps of their subject were very limited. They did not even have to remember the facts in their textbooks, and they had little need to know anything about their subject that was not in the textbook.

CHART curriculum required much more of the teacher. In the CHART model, the written curriculum was only a small part of the knowledge needed. Each teacher had to have a complex mental map that went well beyond the written curriculum. Teachers who had not been through CHART workshops did not have those maps. These maps not only included much more information than teachers traditionally had, but they also included complex new ways of relating and organizing the information.

Wylie (as quoted in Beard, 1992) noted, "Some teachers still have 'very traditional' understandings of what history is, that history is the facts and the names and the dates and the places, and that there are true causes and effects that you can know" (p. 271).

Wylie goes on to say,

> The documentation assumes a common belief in this way of understanding history that may not be there. I don't think it's there among teachers who have not been through the project. We have maybe a third of the teachers who teach world history attached to the project. That's great, but that means that two thirds of the teachers are still out there and that some of those who are attached to the project have internalized it in ways that are more profound than others. (As quoted in Beard, 1992, p. 267)

The Philadelphia project remapped world history from a collection of facts to a collection of pieces of evidence and a method of evaluating and analyzing evidence that led to a constantly changing picture. Instead of seeing history as a final work, participants found history as a self-organizing system in which all of us are components making new history as well as reinterpreting the evidence of the past.

In the hands of a good teacher with adequate knowledge, this model of teaching weaves a web in which students are participating in and creating history as well as evaluating and interpreting the past. In a lesson captured on the videotape, "Fire in Their Eyes" (Javers, 1994), Gloria Barnes begins by asking students what they will tell their grandchildren about the championship ball game that they had seen the previous night. She asks them what artifacts they will save. She leads them to see that they are being historians by preserving and interpreting evidence. She then moves to a discussion of the ways historians interpreted evidence about early humans. Students themselves examine the evidence and then discuss the methods and interpretations of the historians and the way these interpretations changed as new evidence emerged.

The materials on early humans were in the curriculum guide, but Ms. Barnes knew enough additional information that she could let students ask questions that went beyond the information in the book. In addition, she had deep knowledge of her students and their lives, and she knew the methods of historical inquiry well enough that she could weave an original lesson out of the unexpected ideas her students brought up and the information in the historical text.

Developing Depth of Knowledge

The kinds of complex teaching methods CHART was developing not only required extensive knowledge, they also required practice, feedback, and support.

When our institutes taught or demonstrated complex teaching methods, such as portfolio assessment, probing discussion, discovery, simulation, or role playing, I found that a few teachers in each class could use these methods after seeing them modeled once. A few others rejected them immediately.

A significant group, however, imitated the outer form but ignored the analysis and reflection that made the method effective. They would do a simulation game but would ignore the follow-up discussion that developed the concepts. They would do an open-ended discussion that would ramble all over the place with no point or meaning, but they would feel it was good because the students had all participated. Often, the result of partial imitation of a new technique was that students achieved less than they had under more traditional teaching.

Michael Fullan (1991) described this same phenomenon. He noted that teachers have false clarity when they think they have adopted new practices but have just "assimilated the superficial trappings" (p. 35). He noted,

> It is possible to change on the surface by endorsing certain goals, using specific materials, and even imitating the behavior without specifically understanding the principles and rationale of the change. Moreover with reference to beliefs, it is possible to value and even be articulate about the goals of the change without understanding their implications for practice. (p. 40)

Depth Versus False Clarity

For example, in the Arkansas institute in Mexico, we studied the theme of "Identity" in *The Labyrinth of Solitude* by Octavio Paz (1961),

The Death of Artemio Cruz by Carlos Fuentes (1991), and *The Underdogs* by Mariano Azuela (1992). We had lectures and discussions by Mexican professors and visited with and observed Mexicans in a variety of situations, such as a re-creation of the Day of the Dead celebration and a religious festival. Themes emerged and recurred in our informal discussions. The powerful images of tragedy and pessimism from Orozco's murals seemed to capture the basic themes of *The Underdogs* and the frustration of ordinary citizens who talked with us about the economy or the presidential elections. We reflected on the Paz essay on the importance of form as we looked at the structure of the city and as we looked at the characteristics of folk music. Different concepts of time recurred in everyday life and in the structure of the novels.

Although the readings and the exposure to arts and experience had been carefully planned, the important themes and ideas came out of the interaction of the participants, the texts, and real-life experiences under the guidance of the scholars.

All of the teachers who participated recognized that the combination of experience of the culture and academic study created an extremely rich learning experience. But when they attempted to create the same experience in the classroom, many re-created the interdisciplinary structure, but only a few re-created the dialogue and analysis.

The majority succeeded in developing a unit incorporating Mexican literature, art, history, and elements of Mexican culture, such as festivals and dinners. But few were able to integrate the probing questions about identity, time, death, and tragedy that brought significance to the music and literature and cultural experiences. In one school in which Spanish and English classes re-created a Day of the Dead celebration and a Mexican meal, there was a deep discussion of cultural differences, the feelings associated with doing things differently, and the significance of the way a culture deals with death. In another class, doing the same activities, students talked about the basketball game and school gossip while they ate the Mexican dinner.

On the surface, there was not much difference between the two classes. Students in both classes moved about, getting food or examining the Day of the Dead exhibit, writing or talking to each other. By the normally observable and measurable standards, the two classes were doing exactly the same things. One could imagine the same objectives written on the board in both classes: "Students will compare

Mexican and American culture through examining food and a Day of the Dead exhibit and writing their observations." Both classes had high levels of student involvement. Students in both classes were interested and excited. If I had been sitting in the back of the room rating the two classes on most ratings of classroom functioning, they would have rated exactly the same—except on thoughtfulness . . . and very few teacher-rating systems look at thoughtfulness.

The Need for Feedback

Teachers themselves rarely understood the difference between the two kinds of teaching without outside feedback. They tended to be so pleased by the feedback of student interest that they did not notice the lack of complex learning.

I, in fact, didn't notice the difference until Judith Rényi came for a visit and started asking difficult questions. At first, I was not happy with her critique. I was annoyed that she wasn't delighted with the sheer quantity of new lessons and the excitement of students in the classes. It took her quite awhile to train me to listen for depth and analysis and probing questions in addition to interest and excitement. It took me even longer to find ways to provide feedback to volunteer teachers that did not discourage them.

Learning these more complex ways of teaching takes a long time and a lot of feedback. CHART directors estimated that it took 3 years of constant feedback, questioning, and study for most teachers to master the more complex techniques.

As CHART educators gained experience, we recognized that teacher teams that allowed teachers to reflect on their experiences and to share feedback were more important over the life of the project than the initial workshops. We also found that it was important to have outsiders such as university scholars and project evaluators interact with the team. Teams did not like to ask each other hard questions, and they sometimes did not have the perspectives to see subtle differences in quality.

Building Support Teams

Teams were important for feedback but more important for support. Complex learning requires a lot of trial and failure and requires facing a lot of cognitive dissonance.

Gene Maeroff (1988), in a study of CHART's efforts at teacher empowerment, stated that CHART teachers

> were forced to come face to face with the uncomfortable reality of their own limitations. They saw this acknowledgment as a prelude to growth. Once they reconciled themselves to their deficiencies, many began taking painful strides to overcome the shortcomings that teachers often live with for a career. (p. 45)

He wrote,

> Somehow the teacher who is being asked to admit deficiencies and change has to be persuaded that there are rewards to be realized. Otherwise, why put oneself on the spot? Just setting the goal of improved teaching performance without increasing the net benefit to one being asked to make the sacrifice may lead to frustration, low morale, defensive behavior and unhappy consequences. (Maeroff, 1988, p. 46)

Maeroff further noted,

> Because they generally feel that there are no rewards for stretching themselves and trying something new, teachers tend to maintain their routines and not try to make the kind of change. . . . The value of a project like CHART is the incentive it provides. (p. 50)

Budgeting for Change

Developing the skills of a teacher-scholar was a slow and difficult process. CHART teachers and directors usually estimated that it took from 3 to 5 years of intensive work and feedback for most teachers to master the new approach to teaching. While they were learning the new approach, their teaching effectiveness was sometimes lower than it had been when they used less effective approaches that they had already mastered. Furthermore, some teachers failed to master the new methods even after intensive training.

A teacher who lacked the skills and knowledge but tried to adopt CHART methods spread misinformation or imitated only the form or the class deteriorated into chaos. Many teachers who were unsuccessful in using CHART methods were reasonably effective using traditional textbook methods.

The possibility that not all teachers had the capacities to use CHART methods was contrary to the basic beliefs and philosophy of most CHART directors. Most of us initially refused to consider this possibility and assumed that our failure to get all teachers to adopt our new methods was the result of something we were doing wrong. By the final CHART directors' meetings, some of us began to raise this possibility. Some suggested that many teachers who rejected CHART methods were making an accurate assessment of their own capabilities. Others vehemently disagreed and maintained that all teachers with adequate opportunity could learn the new methods. We all agreed, however, that few school districts were willing to invest in adequate opportunity for learning for their teachers.

Educators need to face hard budgeting choices more realistically. The teaching methods CHART advocated were a major improvement over the humanities teaching teachers had been doing before. But CHART was expensive. A CHART program half implemented was usually worse than the program it replaced.

We all know that a luxury automobile is better than a stripped-down used model, but we also know what we can afford. Over and over, I found schools commissioning teaching models that were way beyond their budget. They would spend all of their budget on the plans and have nothing left to implement the plans. In fact, some districts seemed to buy a new set of plans each year and never implement any of them.

An accurate map of the knowledge needed to implement a program can allow more effective budgeting. A school might wisely choose to train a third of its teachers well in a new method instead of giving everyone a piece of training. Or a school might be able to select the teachers who have prerequisite training to make a method work.

Suggestions for Practice

1. Before you agree to implement a new change, get an accurate map of the new knowledge needed to make it work. Find teachers who have implemented the procedure effectively and ask them

probing questions—particularly about their knowledge of their students and their knowledge of the subject and how they developed the knowledge. Observe them teaching, and look at the hidden kinds of knowledge that they have, such as knowledge of their students or knowledge of the subject.

Look at advantages they might have that you do not have. For example, we found that rural teachers in our project seemed to find cooperative learning easier than urban teachers. As we mapped the knowledge needed for cooperative learning more accurately, we realized that rural teachers usually knew a lot more about their students and their families, so they did not have to work to discover student learning styles and interaction patterns. Urban teachers, on the other hand, had access to many more sources of information on their subject areas than many rural teachers.

2. Make sure that training programs deal with the new subject knowledge and new knowledge of students that are required as well as procedures. If you are dealing with new content, be sure that your training program includes new ways of organizing and analyzing the information as well as new facts.

If you are dealing with complex new methods, be sure you include provisions for feedback and support as teachers use the methods in the classroom.

3. Be prepared for a drop in performance while teachers are learning new skills. Create support teams and provide a supportive environment to make people feel more comfortable taking risks.

4. Know your limits and budget. The quality of a teaching method depends on the quality of implementation by the particular teacher. Recognize that pushing people to shift to a new way of teaching or behaving before they have an adequate knowledge base may cause worse teaching instead of better.

5. Don't be disappointed if a training program does not lead to immediate implementation or if new knowledge is not used immediately. Adding to the knowledge pool adds to the capacity of the system and may make future changes possible. Teachers who today wisely decide not to implement a new method because they do not know their 150 students well enough may in the future be in a program where they work intensely with 50 students, and they will have that method in their repertoire.

Chapter Six

Building Teams and Partnerships

If you are wanting to make a significant change in your school, you will probably want to find allies or partners to work with. Reforms that involve more than an individual classroom usually require some kind of group effort. Most large-scale reforms involve team-work, partnerships, committees, or networking.

However, developing effective teams, committees, or partners is not easy. How do you decide whom to involve? How do you keep from interesting the wrong people? How do you organize and motivate a team?

CHART Experiences With Teams and Partnerships

CHART focused on forming three types of collaborative groups: community partnerships involving several institutions, school teams involving several teachers, and multicultural curriculum development teams. We learned a lot about the benefits of partnerships and about pitfalls in partnering we needed to avoid.

Sharing Knowledge and Resources Across Institutions

One of the biggest contributions CHART made to most of the areas in which it worked was in building partnerships to share resources among institutions. A good example of the way the foundation, humanities scholars, and public school people shared knowledge was the Washington, D.C., partnership.

There, foundation resources helped a partnership between the Smithsonian Institution and the Washington, D.C., schools get off the ground. The Smithsonian had a tremendous wealth of material that was not being adequately used, and the teachers in the public schools needed resources.

Maria Marable was hired to develop the relationship. She found that teachers and students were not using Smithsonian resources because they did not find it a friendly place. They were overwhelmed by too many materials. They did not know who to go to for information or what to do with all of the materials that were there.

Marable developed workshops to show teachers what was in the museum, how to access it, and how to use it for hands-on learning. She worked with teachers individually to help them see what resources at the Smithsonian fit into their teaching plans. She stressed getting kids out of the schools and into the museum. She broadened teachers' horizons and focused on getting them to learn how to enhance learning.

For example, an English teacher, Pat Bradford, wanted to teach American literature in a historical context. She and Marable put together a program using the Smithsonian's resources. She brought her class to the Smithsonian, and they went to the exhibit titled "From Field to Factory," which explored the theme of migration. The curator talked about how he had researched that exhibit, discussing his own family's experience and the role of literature in his thinking. Then, the class went to the Museum of American Art and viewed art of the time and portraits of the people they were studying.

One of the largest projects Marable undertook used materials on Duke Ellington, which were donated by his family. Seven schools participated in a partnership with the Smithsonian to develop ways of using this rich collection of materials to teach school subjects. They looked at Ellington's music and his life from different perspectives. They used geography to examine his travels, and history and sociology to interpret his life story. At the culmination of the unit, the Smithsonian hosted a Duke Ellington Youth Festival with students from schools around the city coming together to share their work. It was so successful that it has become an annual event.

The impact of the partnership, however, was greater than the creation of a teaching unit and an annual festival. The teachers developed relationships with the Smithsonian Institution, and when the opportunity was available to design magnet schools, these teachers got on the committees and developed an arts and humanities magnet school that has a very close ongoing relationship with the Smithsonian Institution.

Michael Fullan (1993) emphasizes the importance of external partnerships:

> It is sufficient to note that all the success stories considered in this book are founded on strong ongoing relationships between external support groups and internal teams. . . . There is a ceiling effect to conceptualizing inspiring visions, to investigating and solving problems, to achieving greater and greater competencies, and to engaging in productive relationships, if one does not connect to varied and large networks of others in similar and different pursuits. (p. 87)

Building Teams Within Schools

In addition to building partnerships across institutions, CHART built teams within schools. In New York, CHART built a partnership between the New York Public Schools and the American Forum to provide professional development to prepare teachers for a new world history and culture course required by the New York state curriculum. Instead of involving just social studies teachers, whose course had been changed, project director Jamie Cloud created interdisciplinary teams of social studies, English, and art teachers.

The teachers had to learn how to work together. Cloud (as cited in Beard, 1992) noted that the social studies teachers came into the project knowing that they had to follow the state mandate. They knew that they were going to teach about Africa, Latin America, and the Middle East in the first semester of the ninth grade.

> They were pleased, because they figured that art and English were going to help them do what they had to do. Well, art and English said, "We're not on the planet to help you do what you're supposed to do. How are you going to help us do what we're supposed to do?" That was a very interesting process. This process had to help everyone do what they knew they had to do

on their own and find synergy together at the same time. (Cloud as quoted in Beard, 1992, p. 249)

Cloud (as cited in Beard, 1992) emphasized that teams had to plan very carefully to make a unit meaningful for all disciplines. She found that teachers involved in interdisciplinary units often got sidetracked to unimportant topics. She noted that in one unit there was a great interdisciplinary lesson about sidewalks, but sidewalks are not an important topic to study. They also tried a unit on Puritans, with disappointing results. According to Cloud, "We had an example of Puritan art, Puritan literature, and Puritan history, and all that the kids knew was that they were real sick of Puritans" (as quoted in Beard, 1992, p. 250). Most collaborations, however, led to high-interest, intellectually stimulating units that none of the individuals could have done by themselves.

As Beard (1992) reports, Cloud found that most teams needed an outside facilitator the first time they went through the process.

For example, what usually happens in the first meeting is that the social studies teachers already have the guiding center and the questions. The English and art teachers sit back. I walk in and ask if everyone agrees that they will do everything on Africa, for instance. The English and art teachers will say "no." And I'll say, that is what these questions say. And they'll say, "They didn't ask us." Social studies people are so excited. They think this is for them, since they've got the state mandate. Someone needs to facilitate the discussion, and it shouldn't be the one who is the loudest, which is what usually happens. It's a lot more about group dynamics than the curriculum for awhile, until they get used to it. Fortunately, the material is so well linked that, once they get the human stuff out of the way, it's a snap. (p. 254)

As school teams matured, they played important roles in supporting each other and in providing feedback as teachers tried new materials in their classes. In fact, CHART found regular meetings of school teams so important for change that CHART directors began requiring released time during the school day for team meetings as a condition for schools to participate.

Building Relationships
Across Cultures

Because CHART focused on creating a multicultural curriculum, we tried at every level to create multicultural teams. Where we succeeded, we created dynamic projects. For example, in Arkansas, to design our workshop on teaching about West Africa, we pulled together a team of African immigrants; African, African American, and white scholars; and both African American and white teachers. We wove a rich texture of research from multiple perspectives and hands-on demonstrations of dancing, music, fabrics, and ceremonies. The resulting teaching unit was published and is now widely used around the country.

However, multicultural relationships were not always easy because the ways different ethnic groups should relate to each other is a major national controversy.

The core issue in the ethnic debate came out in a 1991 seminar titled "Education for a Diverse Society." Lucius Outlaw (1991), a philosophy teacher at Haverford College, captured a major theme of the seminar when he said,

> What is really at issue is—Which way, America? Where is this nation going to go? Schools are the primary institutions for social reproduction. So in trying to fashion America in some kind of way we try to fashion our kids, because they will inherit our futures, so schools are a hotly contested area. . . . How you make the schools makes the future. (p. 20)

He continued, "I think we are going through what I would call the loss of enforced consensus, both about the meaning of 'America,' what America is, who's defining America, and who's defining the agenda for America's future" (p. 20).

Outlaw continued,

> What is very much at issue is the very sense we have of being a particular people. . . . What do we have in common in our quest to reconstitute ourselves and our differences, and will there be enough in there for us to come to agreement about how to refashion this nation that will allow us both to preserve ourselves in our differences to some extent, while uniting us in a shared na-

tion? I think that to be one of the oldest philosophical problems ever broached in Western history: unity and difference. As far as I'm concerned there's nothing especially sacred about America, it need not be here tomorrow. Ain't nothing guaranteed about it. The only way that it's sacred is if there is a system that would make it sacred. (p. 21)

Mapping Relationships on the Edge of Chaos

The questions Outlaw was asking were at the core of CHART's work and are at the core of our nation's future. Do we have enough in common to give our allegiance to a multicultural nation, or do our interests really lie with our ethnic groups?

On the map of the edge of chaos, a critical question is, When does a system hold together and create a higher level of complexity and when does it collapse into chaos. In our contemporary world, the nations that have collapsed into chaos have collapsed around ethnic and cultural divisions.

Anthropologist Ruth Benedict (1976) tried to find the critical difference between societies that stayed together peacefully and those that deteriorated into violence. She labeled the critical factor *synergy*. She used the word *synergy* to map social structures in which the group produces more than the individuals would produce separately. This is the way the word *synergy* is usually used—to describe a system in which the whole is greater than the sum of its parts. In her use of the term, however, in a synergistic system, each individual gained more from being a part of the system than the individual would have gained from working alone. Not only did the system as a whole gain, but there was mutual benefit to the individuals.

Benedict (1976) pointed out that complex systems do not work because they are built on altruism but because they make self-interest the same as the common interest. A highly synergistic society is like a joint stock company. There may be great differences in the amount of stock each person has, but all still benefit when the company as a whole benefits. In a synergistic system, cooperation should not only create a larger pie, but each individual should get more than he or she would have had without cooperation (see Figure 6.1).

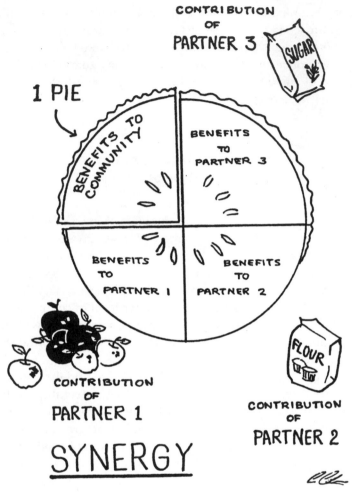

Figure 6.1.

Mapping Mutual Benefit in Partnerships and Teams

Benedict's (1976) concept helps map the problems we frequently found in partnerships and helps explain why some partnerships were successful and others were not.

In the successful partnerships, such as the Smithsonian-public school partnership and the American Forum-school partnership, both partners achieved their core goals. The Smithsonian and American Forum expanded their audiences, and the schools improved their teaching.

In less successful partnerships, the benefits to individual institutions were less clear. For example, the arts in general might be better off for the existence of a partnership, but a particular institution might find that the partnership was draining its resources. When foundation money was available, institutions could easily define a CHART project as part of their mission, but when money became scarce, they would perceive the project as draining resources from their core mission. In Arkansas, the project was initially embraced both by school districts and by the university. However, when budgets became tight, school districts retrenched from interdisciplinary humanities to courses required by state guidelines, and the university focused scarce resources on the education of undergraduates, not service to the public schools. Both the schools and the university liked CHART, but it was not tied directly to the state curriculum, as it was in New York, nor was it part of the core mission of the university.

In building multicultural partnerships, CHART leaders had to convince all groups that they would gain more by working together than each group would gain independently.

Designing Mutual Benefit

Benedict (1976) pointed out that synergy is not something that is automatic. Social structures, within limits, can be designed to maximize synergy or to minimize it. CHART leaders found that many institutions were designed so that people who participated in CHART would not benefit personally as a result of their contributions. For example, almost all of the university faculty who participated in CHART projects told us that they learned a lot from the experience and improved their own teaching. However, the kind of knowledge and the kind of work they did with CHART were not valued on the professional advancement and salary scales of universities. A professor who spent the summer helping teachers develop curriculum on West Africa might even be penalized for not spending that time working on an obscure monograph that only a few hundred people would ever read.

Public schools also do not reward teachers for the kinds of efforts they put into CHART. There are few if any rewards for a teacher who expends the energy necessary to do better than average work. In fact, in many schools, outstanding teachers are punished by jealousy from fellow teachers and extra responsibilities from administrators. Most teachers find it is to their personal advantage to spend their time with their families and friends or even to get a second job instead of spending time preparing for high-quality teaching.

These reward systems are human constructions and can be changed. Our university is now revising its reward system to count the kind of work faculty did with CHART as a scholarly activity. Some states are experimenting with differential pay proposals or re-certification requirements that would reward higher-quality teaching. The current Rockefeller Foundation initiative is examining the staff development programs in larger urban districts to see if they can be restructured to support and reward CHART-like improvements in schools.

Over the years, CHART directors learned to avoid wasting energy on unproductive partnerships. At first, the high energy level and excitement of CHART meetings encouraged people to perceive more potential in relationships than was actually there, and most of us tried to form too many partnerships, teams, and networks.

One of our biggest disappointments was our failure to form a networking strategy to keep CHART directors in contact from sites around the country. Almost every year, when we met together, we came up with a strategy for communicating or for working together that we thought would benefit each project while benefiting the network as a whole. In the late 1980s, before the Internet became widely available, we tried to set up several versions of computer networking systems. They always sounded very good when we were at a national meeting with computer experts demonstrating the systems, but they became a major drain on local resources when we found out the local costs of computer equipment, phone lines, and the skills needed to run them.

We learned to estimate the costs of partnerships and to choose not to invest in unpromising partnerships. Initially, we were so committed to partnering and teamwork that we formed partnerships and teams that had no potential for working, partners where team members would have to invest far more than they could hope to gain.

Initially, many of us in CHART assumed that the more partners, the better. And with Rockefeller Foundation prestige and money as a stimulus, creating partnerships was deceptively easy. When the

Rockefeller Foundation came to a city such as Little Rock, everyone was eager to get involved. However, not everyone turned out to have something useful to contribute or a motive for wanting to. Those who had the most to contribute often had strong and sometimes contradictory ideas about what should be done with their resources. Maintaining partnerships turned out to be quite time consuming, and not all of them proved to be worth the trouble. My observations suggest that on the institutional level, two or three partners seemed to be most effective, and on the individual level, school teams of four to six teachers and one or two outside resource people. Most of us initially pictured partnerships as a source of resources, not as consumers of resources. When we mentally mapped partnerships, we looked only at the resources each institution could bring to the partnership. We initially did not consider the costs in time and resources required to maintain partnerships. We soon learned that collaboration is very time consuming. Several of us went through a brief phase where project activity and fund-raising almost stopped while we went to endless meetings with partners. Partnerships and networks compete for resources with other activities of an individual or an organization.

Andy Hargreaves (1994), in his research on teachers' perceptions of their work, noted that teachers often perceive costs to teaming and partnership that administrators are not aware of. He distinguishes collaboration from contrived collegiality in which collaboration is compulsory, administratively regulated, and implementation oriented. He found that teachers may see time spent in collaboration as time lost with kids.

Strategies for Forming Effective Partnerships and Teams

1. Carefully choose a limited number of partners. As a general rule, teachers seemed to be able to work most productively with one in-school team and one outside partner at a time. Partnerships need to be voluntary, and they need to be supported by the school with time and space. If the participants do not see their value, they will waste time. If the school does not see a value to the team or partnership, it is likely to run into barriers in trying to achieve its goal.

2. Examine what each partner will gain. Discuss carefully with potential partners what they hope to gain from the partnership. Discuss why they consider it important and how it ties to their core mission. Sometimes, you will find that potential partners have vague or unrealistic goals. Goals of potential partners may even conflict. It is better to find out that you have little to gain from working together or that your goals are not compatible before you invest much in the partnership.

Make sure the partnership goals are tied to the core goals of each partner or team member. Sometimes, for example, we had teachers who wanted to join a team because they had a strong personal interest in global or multicultural education even though their teaching specialty had little relationship to the topic. Sometimes, such a person made a major contribution to the team, but more frequently, we invested too much energy in training a person who could not use the training.

3. Examine the costs of teaming and partnership. Budget accurately the time and resources required for the partnership to work. In deciding whether to start a partnership, consider the opportunity costs. How else could that time be invested, and what will you lose by not investing it in the other activities?

4. Look for ways of creating synergy. Examine ways of restructuring time and reward systems to make a partnership more synergistic. Recognize that as times change, institutions shift resources and priorities, so a relationship that was unproductive at one time may be more productive another.

5. Develop the human dimensions of a partnership. The rewards of a partnership are often more in pleasure, recognition, and relationships than they are in material gain or achievement of goals. The Smithsonian Duke Ellington Festival created rewards of recognition and the excitement of a large festival. Although material benefits are hard to expand, social benefits are infinitely expandable. We found it was important to make CHART meetings fun and rewarding. A small investment in social amenities often created a big increase in the benefits people felt from participating in partnerships.

Chapter Seven

Charting Conflict

Your school reform project will probably start with a group of very nice, very enthusiastic people working together for a common goal. After all, you've selected each other as partners.

However, before too long, these nice people are likely to turn into angry and frustrated people. Or, they may stay nice and polite but quit coming to the meetings.

If you are working on a significant school reform, you can almost promise yourself that you will encounter conflict. And the way your group handles conflict will be one of the most important factors deciding whether you succeed or fail.

Why do school reforms run into conflict? What role does conflict play in school reform? How can reformers manage conflict to create effective change?

The Roles of Conflict in Self-Organizing Systems

One of the most important ways that most of us have to revise our mental maps is in the way we see conflict. On our old maps, a conflict is a warning sign. It shows that we have hit a wall, and in a stable system, we cross walls at our own peril. In other words, we detect the constraints in a society because we hit conflicts when we reach them. Most people see conflicts as signals that they need to rethink their choices. Conflict is evidence that you are doing something that doesn't fit the system.

However, if you want to change a system, conflict provides your opportunity. In complex, changing systems, new structures grow from conflict. If you are changing a system, you have to move the walls, and the way you move them is through conflict.

Self-organizing systems are possible because the components have choices, and in every choice there is an element of conflict. Self-organizing systems adapt because new information or environmental changes conflict with old structures. Potential new structures compete with each other. Darwin saw competition or conflict as the only force driving natural selection and evolution. Contemporary self-organizing systems theories point out other factors at work, as well, but still describe the essential role of conflict in creating and maintaining complex structures.

In system change, conflict is one of the major mechanisms of change. People do not trust a new shape until they have gone through conflicts. They do not know where the new attractors or constraints are until a conflict has made them visible and shown their power. They will not cross old boundaries until they find through conflict that the barrier is weakened or down.

There are two main kinds of conflicts in system change. The first is perspective conflict, which contributes new knowledge. The second is power conflicts, which actually restructure the system.

Charting Perspective Conflicts

One of the main reasons for conflict in system change is multiple perspectives. Each person sees the world through the lenses of his or her own experience, institutional roles, and cultural background. As we saw in Chapter 1, different cultures map the world differently, and each map lets us see different dimensions of society.

We also have different maps based on our institutional affiliations and our roles in the institutions. Our mental maps have our own institutions at the center and our own tasks or goals well focused. For example, a museum educator is likely to see the museum at the center of a collaborative project and to see the purpose of the project as bringing children to use the existing museum resources. A teacher, however, may see her unique children at the center of her world and may see the museum as a distant, hard-to-get-to place with exhibits that will not interest children. A university scholar is likely to see knowledge about literature or history at the center of the project and to have little interest or concern about the needs of children or about the museum.

For the partnership to be effective, these mental maps have to be shared, and each partner has to adjust his or her mental image to include the visions of the others. This process enriches everyone and multiplies the total pool of knowledge. One of the fastest ways to increase your knowledge is to spend some time seeing through another person's eyes. In a complex system, no one can see the whole; the closest we can come is to see it from many different perspectives.

Contemporary theories of learning show conflict as central to the learning process. Piaget (as cited in Wadsworth, 1978) saw a mental conflict or cognitive dissonance between two sets of information as the primary motivation for developing more sophisticated schemata.

Perspective conflicts are best dealt with by making sure that everyone has plenty of opportunity to listen to all points of view and has time to discuss and adjust their mental maps to incorporate the new information. It is important to recognize that another perspective adds new information, even though initially it seems to only bring frustration, as illustrated in Figure 7.1.

A CHART Project Learns From a Perspective Conflict

The Connecticut Humanities Council coordinated a project that involved a partnership between the council, several local school districts, and various universities and museums. Before joining CHART, they had funded summer institutes of 4 to 6 weeks—university or museum based.

Jane Christie, director of the Council, first became involved with CHART as a source of knowledge and information. In an interview, Christie (personal communication, March 1995) said,

I read an article by Judith Rényi about PATHS and what they were doing in museums. So I stopped by when I was in Philadelphia to pick her brain about school collaboration. We asked her advice and invited her up to speak to us on Professional Development.

Figure 7.1.

When CHART expanded, Rényi encouraged the Connecticut council to apply to join.

Christie (personal communication, March 1995) remembers,

> Initially, there was quite a difference in perspective between the Connecticut Humanities Council and CHART. Our goal for teachers was quite narrow. CHART broadened all our thinking. We wanted teachers to know the content of the disciplines and bridge the gap between university scholarship and what we saw

happening in the classroom and the textbook. We assumed that the scholars know the scholarship, the teachers know about curriculum, and if we bring them together they will know what to do. In some cases that was true, but not very often. We had a group of 10 or 20 teachers enjoying what we were doing, but it was not having any impact in the schools.

Our thinking has changed. I thought if teachers can only hear lectures and read current books, this is what they need. I imagined that teachers were eager to read stuff and play with it with their students. I had no idea of the range of challenges that teachers face in their classes or of the weakness of their academic background.

Initially we tried to have teachers and scholars develop curriculum. We had the scholars speak in the morning. The teachers never took a note. Then in the afternoon they sat down to write the curriculum, but what they wrote didn't relate to the lectures at all. We expected them to hear four or five big ideas, but they would pick an obscure statement that for some reason resonated, leaving out the major ideas. It was bizarre.

When we taught a book, teachers did not see the same things in it that scholars did. The low point in the project for me was when we had a book about European history 1100-1300 that looks at the Mediterranean as a center of civilization. It was interesting interpretation, very fertile for rethinking the world history curriculum. We had teachers reading. We thought new ideas would come out. But they repeated facts. They told facts. None of them mentioned the interpretation. They went back over a series of facts. We didn't know what to do.

We gradually realized that there was a lot more to changing teaching in the humanities than letting scholars lecture at the teachers. We got into a thousand things we never intended, from relationships with school districts to working on performance-based assessment. We never would have thought that was part of our agenda—we thought it was a teachers' problem.

We evolved from institutes to curriculum workshops to action research teams reflecting on their teaching. In the last few years we've had curriculum leadership teams . . . all these were needed to help teachers develop and keep collaboration going. We now have laboratory schools. These were all things originally dismissed as pedagogical and unrelated to the goals of the

Humanities Council. We realized that we couldn't do "pure" humanities. The seeds were falling on infertile soil if we didn't do the other stuff.

Our board has changed from seeing ourselves as a mini-National Endowment for the Humanities to having interest in systemic impact. They are interested in institutionalization, longevity of programs and approaches. Our board has changed. We now have more people who are involved with elementary and secondary education. Everyone who participated in the project has found that their ideas have changed dramatically, but the process of growth has taken a lot of time.

Charting Coevolution

As Christie (personal communication, March 1995) pointed out, participating in a partnership changed the knowledge base of all participants and changed the structures of both institutions. Scholars learned to see education differently, and teachers learned to see new dimensions of the disciplines.

Christie (personal communication, March 1995) relates, "Most of us initially mapped the partnership as something outside our institution which we could participate in without making internal changes." In many of the successful partnerships, the expanded vision provided by the partnership reshaped the partner institutions.

Biologists call the process of organisms influencing each others' evolution *coevolution.* A parallel process often occurred at CHART. Often, universities or museums joined projects with the idea that they were going to make changes in schools, but most of them found themselves making at least as many changes in their own institutions.

"We've been successful," Christie (personal communication, March 1995) says.

> We have sort of a solution, but it is so labor intensive and takes such a long time of ongoing collaboration that it is not practical for all schools. People who have been 5 or 6 years in the project are now beginning to say, "Oh, now I see why you suggested that a long time ago," but where do you get the resources to support teachers and scholars working collaboratively for 5 or 6 years?

Charting Power Conflicts

Perspective conflicts such as those Jane Christie dealt with were opportunities for both groups to expand their mental maps. Working through perspective conflicts creates synergy because both parties gain information and develop expanded, more accurate, and more powerful mental maps. Sharing information creates more information, so working through a perspective conflict leaves everyone with more knowledge.

Not all conflicts, however, are over expandable resources, such as knowledge. Conflicts that restructure access to scarce resources usually do not have a win-win solution. These power conflicts usually have clear winners and losers. Power conflicts are much more intractable than perspective conflicts, and many CHART members continued to see them as unproductive. However, power conflicts are very important in changing a system because it is these conflicts that actually create changes in structure (see Figure 7.2).

The Role of Power Conflicts in System Change

My map of the role of conflict in system change came from working with my late husband, Gene Stanford, and his collaborator, Al Roark, as they studied the way classroom groups change from being teacher centered to student centered. His research was stimulated by theory and techniques from the training groups of Jack Gibb (Stanford, 1990; Stanford & Roark, 1974).

Jack Gibb's training seminars introduced us to the concept of self-organizing groups that could develop sophisticated patterns of interaction and problem solving by allowing leadership functions to emerge from the group. We tried to create more complex patterns of interaction in our classrooms that would allow us to push students to higher levels of thinking. Stanford and Roark (1974) discovered that classrooms in which students took responsibility and became actively involved in constructing the course as well as their own learning passed through several stages.

During the first stage, people became acquainted and developed enough knowledge of each other and enough trust to become more personally involved with each other. Initially, the group functioned at a low level of interaction, with almost all interaction controlled by

"TWO PEOPLE MOVING A WALL"

Figure 7.2.

the teacher. Students chose to keep a low profile and to interact only in "safe" ways while they gathered information about how much the group could be trusted.

A teacher who wanted to develop a self-regulating class deliberately disrupted that first structure by leading the students through interactions that built trust, that increased information about the various group members, and that gave them opportunities to test reactions.

During the second stage, the students needed to develop a set of group norms, such as cooperation, responsibility, procedures for making decisions, and dealing with conflict.

At some point toward the end of the norm development stage, when everyone understands the norms and is intellectually committed to them, there is usually a period of conflict. Jack Gibb pointed out that these conflicts are usually ostensibly about something else, but the real issue is leadership and power. Sometimes, they turn into a "Get the leader" hostility. The real question is whether the more democratic structures will work or whether the leader will revert to authoritarian procedures or the group will collapse into chaos. The conflict tests the new norms that until then had been only words.

Frequently, there is a fairly clear phase transition marked by a serious conflict or a series of conflicts as the class moves from a teacher-dominated system to a system in which self-organization plays a greater role.

These conflicts have two functions. First, they open the system to a flood of new knowledge as the anger and frustration generated by the conflict give people the energy to break previous boundaries of acceptable knowledge, and they flood the system with the information from previously hidden perspectives. All of the thoughts that fear or politeness had kept hidden come pouring out. Second, the conflicts establish new boundaries and shift power and responsibility. A skillful teacher guides students through the trial-and-error phase of testing new relationships and leads them to a new regime.

The conflict stage can be dangerous. As Prigogine (Prigogine, Gregoire, & Babloyants, 1972b) noted of chemical self-organizing systems, the results of a phase transition were not completely controllable. However, we found that if we prepared the group ahead of time with listening, organization, and conflict management skills, those skills would shape the way the group would reorganize, and it would almost always reach a higher level of functioning. The new listening, organization, and conflict management skills were tested in the fire of conflict and locked in and shaped the new level of functioning.

A class that had gone through this phase transition suddenly functioned with a much higher level of intelligence than the same group had shown previously. The same people could solve both subject matter and interpersonal problems they could not solve 2 weeks earlier. But this intelligence belonged to this specific group. If we

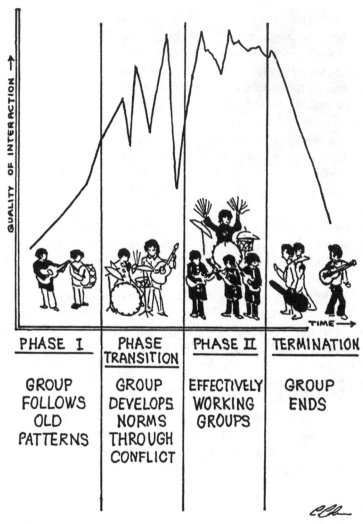

Figure 7.3.

reshuffled students who had developed self-organizing classes into different classes, we had to start over. It was not as hard. We did not have to spend as much time teaching skills, but each group had to go through the stages of trust building and conflict to reach its potential.

A group that successfully dealt with conflict functioned on a much higher level until a couple of weeks before the termination of the group, when people experienced sadness at leaving a close-knit support group (see Figure 7.3).

This model has much in common with the models of how self-organizing systems reorganize to a higher level. As the model predicts, a group has to go through a period of disruption before a more complex system can be developed. However, the Stanford and Roark (1974) model suggests that humans can strongly influence the restructuring that occurs during the conflict or chaos stage by providing the group with knowledge and skills needed by the more sophisticated structure before the conflict stage is reached.

The Conflict Phase in CHART Projects

As CHART moved from classroom changes to larger-scale restructuring, the stages that Stanford and Roark (1974) found in classrooms seemed also to appear in schools and school districts. Dr. Rényi saw a recurring pattern in CHART conflicts. The different partners in projects generally worked well together as long as the projects were limited enough not to affect power issues. However, as the projects became larger and more successful and began to involve school restructuring, both the district partners and the local education funds tended to back away. School administrators, who supported small-scale projects to improve the humanities, became less friendly when the projects began to involve teacher empowerment and teacher involvement in decision making or to require changes in the school schedule. In at least one district, a superintendent who started out supporting the project became actively hostile when the project began to promote restructuring.

Power conflicts were the barrier on which many CHART projects foundered. That should not be surprising. Power conflicts are where new structures and ideas are tested against each other and against the original system. Power conflicts are the way a system restructures. Power conflicts test whether a new structure is truly synergistic. If it is synergistic, even though some people will lose relative power, they will gain more than they had in the old system even if they lose power or resources in a particular area. If the system is not synergistic, there will be clear winners and losers, and the power struggle will show who the losers are going to be. Typically, in a voluntary partnership, the potential loser takes the opportunity of pulling out. Unfortunately, the "fittest" survivor of a power struggle is not necessarily the champion of the best idea or structure. The kind of people who are good at creating new ideas in classrooms are often not very good in power struggles. Even today, CHART leaders differ in their views of whether CHART should focus on changing school systems or should avoid power conflicts by limiting its goals to creating a space within schools for creativity.

Not all power struggles are productive. Sometimes, partnerships were simply frustrated by turf battles or by individuals seeking to enhance their own power at the expense of the project. "At times of reform and change," James Floyd, an Arkansas principal, pointed out, "there are shifts of power and power vacuums. Some people see the opportunity to grab power that they are unable to use wisely. People who first embrace change often have the wrong motives— they are often looking for power."

Resolving Power Conflicts Successfully

Working through the power conflicts was essential to successfully maintaining partnerships as well as making internal changes. Pulaski Heights Junior High School in Little Rock was one of the schools that was most successful at maintaining partnerships and at restructuring. They were partners both in CHART and in New Futures for Little Rock Youth, funded by the Annie Casey Foundation, and they had a number of local partnerships. About the third year of the project, a team of teachers attended our workshop on team building. We spent most of our time discussing their conflict with the principal, who had seemed such a wonderful person before they started restructuring. They were frustrated because they seemed to have constant conflicts with him.

Simply remapping conflict changed the whole situation. They had seen conflict as evidence that something was wrong, as evidence that someone was a bad person or doing bad things. When they learned to see conflict as the equivalent of sore muscles after starting a new exercise program, they could laugh about it. They recognized that the conflicts were the result of the principal shifting decision-making powers to them. But the new limits had to be set up and tested by conflict.

We practiced skills of conflict management: active listening, assertive confrontation, negotiation, and mediation. With these kinds of skills, the teachers were able to work through the conflicts productively.

After surviving the period of conflict, Pulaski Heights, which has now survived a change in leadership, became one of the state models of a restructured school that seem to have stabilized on the new model.

In an effectively synergistic system, power issues are more likely to be resolvable with collaborative conflict management methods. In a nonsynergistic system, they are resolved by force and power.

Strategies for Managing Conflict

1. Be prepared for conflict. Discuss the role of conflict in the change process when you first initiate the change, and remind yourself and others when it happens. When conflict comes, recognize it as an opportunity.

2. Develop your skills in advance. Solving conflicts creatively requires five basic steps. A number of training programs are available to teach groups how to resolve conflicts. Many schools now have a peer mediator program, and the processes peer mediators use are close the to processes faculty members need to use. Student mediators, of course, are inappropriate for resolving faculty conflicts, but the people who train and supervise peer mediators may also be able to provide faculty training. The basic skills of conflict management are the same. Popular secondary conflict management training manuals, such as Copeland's (1989) *Managing Conflict* or Sadalla, Henriquez, and Holmberg's (n.d.) *Conflict Resolution,* contain concepts and activities that are also useful with adults.

Before people reach the conflict stage, they need to be prepared for it. In my experience, the most important and the simplest way to productive conflict management is to introduce a group very early to a simple conflict management procedure and to get the group's agreement to use it. The steps to the procedure should be either posted in the meeting room or readily available on an overhead projector transparency or flip chart so they can be pulled out as needed. The basic steps should be something like the following:

a. The whole group reviews the procedure and agrees to follow it

b. Each group with a distinctive point of view has an opportunity to fully explain that point of view. The explanation should be as clear as possible and should avoid attacks or blame.

c. Each group should listen to each other group and should summarize the other group's point of view to make sure that they understand it correctly.

d. Then, the total group should brainstorm ways that every group's needs can be met.

e. The total group should make a decision about the solution that comes closest to meeting all groups' needs.

f. The agreement should be written, and after about 2 weeks, the group should check back to make sure it is satisfactory.

If the conflict is severe, a mediator or facilitator may be needed. A mediator does not make a judgment about the conflict but simply helps people follow the agreed-on procedure. The procedure is hard to follow for people who are angry and upset. Find the most skillful facilitators you can to help you resolve the conflict. Many communities have mediation programs with trained mediators available.

Chapter Eight

Monitoring Results

If you are trying to make changes in schools, you need feedback to find out if you are being successful. In a complex system undergoing rapid change, finding out the results of your actions is not easy. As we have seen in previous chapters, complex systems have feedback loops instead of simple cause-and-effect relationships. Immediate success is not a good predictor of long-term success, and small-scale reforms do not necessarily work at a larger scale.

How do you find out if your reforms are successful? How do you provide feedback to others, and how do you avoid being overwhelmed by unnecessary and useless assessments?

The Role of Feedback and Assessment in Self-Organizing Systems

Feedback is central to the structure of a self-organizing system. Most of the attractors and constraints in a human system emerge as we try out a behavior and find out what kind of response we get. We adapt as we get information that our actions are having results we do not want.

However, assessment on a self-organizing system map is very different than the vision of assessment on our old maps that assumed there was some kind of control center. From about 1960 to 1980, state departments of education and school districts tried to follow industrial models and to control behavior by setting up reward-and-punishment systems based on objective tests. Because these assessment systems were based on inaccurate maps, they often locked in outdated curricula and encouraged maladaptive decisions from the people whose choices were most critical.

A CHART School Faces a Dysfunctional Assessment System

I visited a CHART school shortly after the largest newspaper in the state had published the test scores of every school district in the state, and their district had distributed results by school and teacher. Their scores were reasonably good, but the principal wanted them to be at the top.

"I'm convinced that we have the best social studies program in the state," said Ms. P., one of the CHART teachers, "but the tests don't show it." She went on to say,

> We were one of the first elementary schools to have a social stud-ies program, so we designed our own curriculum, which we have perfected for a number of years. I'm convinced it is much better than the new state curriculum, but unfortunately, the new test doesn't match our program. We had Africa in the sixth grade. They put it in the fourth and test for knowledge of Africa at the end of the fourth grade when our students have been studying China.
>
> Furthermore, the test just asks for facts. Our children know facts, but they know a lot more. They understand sophisticated concepts about culture, diversity, migration. They know how to analyze information. But none of those skills show up on the test. The test does not let them show what they know that other schools are not teaching.

I asked,"What will you do to improve test scores?"
Mrs. P. laughed,

> Well, you know, the easiest way to change your average test scores is to get the bottom kids in your school transferred to a rival school, or suspend them or get them put into special education. We haven't gotten orders like that yet, but I have heard rumors of teachers encouraging certain children to be sick on test day.

"What we'll really do," said Mrs. P., "is throw out our carefully refined curriculum and adopt the inferior state curriculum."

"Won't you do anything to improve your teaching to raise test scores?" I asked.

"Of course not," she replied.

This is a minimum performance test. To improve our test scores, we need to do a worse job of teaching! We will have to quit spending time on teaching students to think and focus on making them memorize facts that they will soon forget and teaching them how to fill out bubbles on an answer sheet.

Then we'll ignore our best students. The top two thirds of the class will pass this text without any help. We'll cut out all the rigorous and enriched teaching that challenges the best students and drill that bottom third of the class on the facts that the test will cover. After the test is over, we can spend April and May teaching a couple of rich and rigorous CHART units—except that our students will be trained not to think by that time.

Developing an Effective Assessment System for a Rapidly Changing Society

Unfortunately, Mrs. P.'s analysis of teachers' response to minimum performance tests was pretty accurate. Fortunately, she and her CHART team responded differently. They became actively involve in designing an alternative assessment procedure.

An effective feedback and assessment program for a self-organizing system needs to have the following characteristics:

1. It needs to give results to the people who make the critical decisions.
2. It needs to give feedback on the real goals.
3. It needs to provide feedback from multiple perspectives, and it needs to encourage the development of professional judgment.
4. It needs to avoid time-wasting and distracting assessments.

Providing Results to the People Who Make the Decisions

In 1985, the Rockefeller Foundation promoted a collaborative effort between the Pittsburgh Public Schools, Harvard Project Zero, and Educational Testing Service to develop an approach to assessment that would enable teachers to look at the kinds of learning that are important in the humanities.

They recognized that the person who most needs feedback is the student because the student has the most power to decide what and how to improve.

The Pittsburgh project used a portfolio approach in which students keep representations of their works from beginning to final stage and their reflections on their work at various stages of progress. Students periodically sort their materials and select those they want to keep and those they want to discard. Students are encouraged to discuss their works with each other, the teacher, and sometimes with parents who provide additional feedback. Teachers, other students, and parents were encouraged to respond as a real audience, sharing their reactions to the work instead of grading it on arbitrary criteria.

The process focuses on developing the students' power of self-evaluation and the student's skill and comfort at using feedback and criticism from teachers and other audiences. Although the teacher usually retains ultimate control over the grade, the student usually has some input into it.

At its best, the portfolio process sets in motion a set of positive feedback activities that lead to a profound change in the culture and activities of the classroom. As teacher Kathryn Howard (1993) describes it,

> Students and teachers essentially became co-discoverers, working together to identify and explore those strategies that most effectively improved the students' understanding and assessment of their writing and their writing growth. The results of the classroom implementation were then discussed again, modified, and refined as the research continued. (pp. 89-90)

Providing Feedback on the Real Goals

One of the biggest flaws in the kind of assessment system Mrs. P. faced was that the goals it defined were not closely related to the goals of a good teacher. Leaders of the CHART educators in Pittsburgh started by trying to define learning in the arts. Quite clearly, it is not just adding a bunch of new information. In the arts, finding and defining interesting problems is at least as important as answering questions. Young artists need to develop their own standards and critical judgment instead of relying on teacher answers or an answer key. In the arts, development of a product often occurs over a period of time. The finished product shows only a small part of the process (Wolf,1987/1988).

In the Arts-Propel model of arts education, students were to improve their skills of perceiving their own and other works, of producing works of art, and of reflecting on their productions. In other words, they were looking at knowledge as a component of the act of creation. The skills they were developing involved active interaction with the world and adaptations based on their observations.

Recognizing the Importance of Multiple Perspectives and Professional Judgment

The portfolio assessment process gave students feedback from a variety of people, each of whom might see different dimensions of the work. Students also learned that not all feedback was equally valid and that learning to give good feedback is an important skill. One of Howard's (1993) eighth grade students, Cara Rubinsky, describes the way they learned to critique each other's work:

The first time we got into groups to revise, no one wanted to make comments. We were afraid to write on one another's papers. But little by little, everyone began to feel more comfortable with each other. After switching revision partners for a few assignments, everyone sort of found their 'niche' and at the same time found a partner on their level who could work constructively with them. . . . We began trading papers, enlarging revision groups to make the maximum use of everybody's talent. And that's the best way to write. (p. 95)

We discovered that the new forms of assessment that we were developing required of the teachers a much deeper subject matter knowledge than the old forms and deeper skills at assessment. Tom Brewer, formerly of the University of Arkansas at Little Rock Art Department, worked with Gibbs Elementary School to develop a performance assessment test of geography and world culture knowledge, using student art. He had students do before-and-after drawings

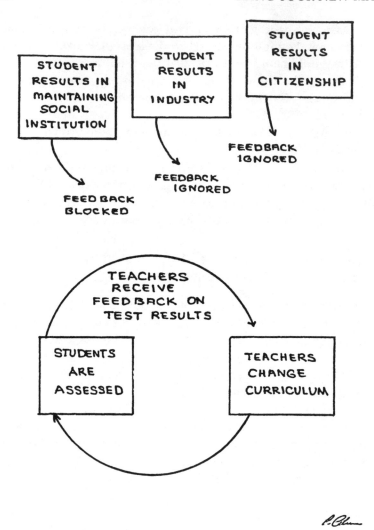

Figure 8.1.

and taught the teachers to analyze the elements of the drawings using a technique that included making a holistic rating, counting the number of symbols, evaluating the accuracy of the symbols, observing the sophistication of the figures (gingerbread figures vs. stick figures), and observing whether there was interaction or individual activity.

As teachers began to use the assessments, they found that they needed much greater knowledge of the cultures they were studying. Children would add a lot to the pictures from their imaginations, and teachers had to do additional research to find out if they were right. Students, for example, often incorporated children playing into their drawings. Teachers learned that this was a topic that interested children, but they had to do more research to incorporate it accurately.

Eliminating Unnecessary and Distracting Assessments

It is important to eliminate time-consuming and distracting assessments. At worst, they distract attention from the important feedback (see Figure 8.1).

The Soviet Union collected massive feedback about achievement of 5-year plans, but this feedback distorted the system's capacity to recognize market trends and significant technological changes.

An assessment system designed from mechanical system maps is static and sets up communication that blocks awareness of change or focuses attention on insignificant aspects of the system. It sets up artificial attractors that block communication that tells the system what adaptations are needed for survival and success. An industrial-model assessment system distorts the landscape of attractors, encouraging people to choose inappropriate shortcuts, such as those Ms. P. described.

Suggestions for Designing Your Assessment System

1. Decide who make the decisions that are most important, and think about what information they need.

2. Think carefully about what your real goal is.

3. Recognize the value of multiple perspectives and of professional judgment.

4. Eliminate unnecessary assessments.

Chapter Nine

Deepening Roots in a Swirling World

If you are over 30, you were probably socialized for a stable world. You were probably taught habits and ideals that help you fit into a bureaucracy. In kindergarten, you learned to eat and go to the bathroom by the clock. In first grade, you learned to sit in a seat for long periods of time. In the upper grades, you not only learned a set of mental maps for a stable world, but you probably also leaned values and emotions, such as institutional loyalty and respect for authorities, that helped you get ahead in a stable, bureaucratic world. You probably also learned ways to find satisfaction and pleasure in a clearly defined and regulated workplace.

How can we adapt to a rapidly changing world, and how should we socialize our children to adapt? Many of our traditional values are under siege from changing lifestyles, from the media, and from social pressures. Which of these values and ideals were simply ways of adapting to an era that has passed and what are the enduring values that make life worth living? What social customs need to be discarded in a multicultural, electronic age, and what courtesies and civilities are essential to holding a society together?

CHART Probes Basic Values Questions

These questions are the core of the arts and the humanities, and CHART teachers found that the more children's lives became disrupted, the more important it became to offer both teachers and students the opportunity to explore these questions through the arts and humanities.

Understanding Our Past

"I used to define the humanities as 'the great achievements of mankind' when I was trying to recruit students and their parents," said Neil Anstead of the Los Angeles Project, HUMANITAS. "I've changed that to include not only the achievements but the limitations of mankind" (as quoted in Beard, 1992, p. 52).

He continued,

> No matter where I go there are some very ugly issues. The roots of prejudice are very, very deep. We have a unit on that, and when I discuss it with people they say that there's nothing bright in it. They have to have this sort of silver lining to everything. A great fear of saying anything to the students, that there are real negative forces in the world and they are in you too and in me. We work at controlling these, but let's face the fact that they are there. (as quoted in Beard, 1992, p. 51)

Adolescents tend to have very limited mental maps, with their own local problems at the center of the world. Our technological society also tends to encourage shallow maps, with science providing quick and easy solutions to all our problems. Science found a vaccine and eliminated polio. Science put men on the moon. As we observed successes of science and of U.S. military and political power in the first half of the century, we drew mental maps that showed scientific research as omniscient and the U.S. government as omnipotent. Those mind maps led us to assume that poverty could be eliminated in a decade. They led us to assume that not only segregation but prejudice and racism could be eliminated by government edict. They continue to lead us to hope that schools and classrooms can be transformed with a simple formula that will make it easy to teach well and will guarantee success to all students.

Through a humanities program, such as the CHART program in Los Angeles, teachers and young people encounter people from distant historical periods and distant cultures who faced similar problems. By studying art, literature, and history, students can develop deep reservoirs of human experiences and images of the actions and ideals that have been valued and the choices that have led to disaster and disgrace. Both teachers and students develop strength and wisdom dealing with a world in which there are not always answers, in which it has never been easy to be good, and in which the inevitable end of both our lives and our dreams is death. CHART teachers, like Anstead quoted earlier, knew that power and creativity come out of pain and that a curriculum that ignores evil and suffering diminishes our capacity for greatness.

The new scientific maps probe more deeply and demonstrate the limits of science. As self-organizing-systems researchers learn to use multiple perspectives and to look back over geological, biological, and human evolution, they are recognizing the limits of scientific solutions.

Stuart Kauffman (1995) writes,

As if by an invisible hand, each adapting species acts according to its own selfish advantage, yet the entire system appears magically to evolve to a poised state where, on average, each does as best as can be expected. Yet, each is eventually driven to extinction, despite its own best efforts, by the collective behavior of the system as a whole. (p. 27)

Making Choices for Our Future

Throughout human history, the self-reinforcing engines of technology have been so powerful that they have driven cultural change. The inventions of fire, baskets, weapons, agriculture, wheels, and assembly lines pushed humans to reorganize their lifestyles. But not all technological changes led to successful societies. Around the planet are the wrecks of towns burned because their fires got out of control, cities in ruins because their agricultural practices exhausted the soil or destroyed because their weapons undermined their political structures.

Human societies that have survived and have lived well have learned to manage their technology. Their artists, writers, and performers have identified problems and have mobilized support for moral and legal walls or economic barriers to harmful practices.

Religion, philosophy, and the arts remind us that there are important values in our lives that machines and technology cannot fulfill and that we have choices about the way we spend our time and our resources.

Our schools and the rest of our society are probably going to be restructured over the next decade whether we like it or not. We are making choices every day that will influence the way they are shaped. We need to set up constraints and attractors to make sure that the new shapes are based on the needs of children for a nurturing environment that will develop their capacities in the arts and will build a rich enough store of stories and history to give them a sense of who they are and where they want to go.

As human beings gain more and more control over our planet's ecosystem and perhaps even our solar system, our vision of our role in the universe, our ideals of the good and the beautiful, and our taboos will decide which species survive and which become extinct, what molecules are created, and how the land masses of our world are shaped.

As we hold in our hands the powerful technology that we have created, we cannot simply make the easy choices, do what comes naturally, or follow the path of least resistance. We have created a world that suspends the laws of evolution. We deliberately preserve the unfit. We bulldoze the fit and the unfit alike. We breed plants and animals to meet our needs, our values, or our sense of beauty. We reshape the landscape, redirect the flows of water, and modify the weather. We struggle against the laws of nature.

Making water flow uphill was one of the primary motives for the evolution of complexity in early civilizations. Most early civilizations coalesced around activities such as making canals or irrigation ditches or wells to change and maintain the changed flow of water.

The cultural heroes of most societies have been people who go uphill, who struggle against the natural order. In the Hebrew story, Moses led his people out of civilization and into the desert. For 40 years, he struggled against a people who kept sliding downhill, back into "the fleshpots of Egypt" or into the religions and cultures of neighboring people. In the Greek story, Odysseus resisted one temptation after another, determined to return home against all of the powers of nature and its creatures. Anansi the Spider in African stories and Coyote in Native American stories use the cleverness of their minds to wrest fire and stories from the gods. The story of the United States, from the founding fathers to the civil rights movement, has been a story of struggles against unjust social and political structures.

For a few decades, many of us were able to settle into a period of stability that did not require us to think deeply or to make difficult choices. We are now being pushed to the edge of chaos.

The edge of chaos is not a comfortable place for most people. Most of us prefer comfort and security in our real world and like to confine our chaos to the television or video screen. Our biological instincts seem to pull us toward simple structures. We feel comfortable sitting in the herd and staying out of the way of the leaders who are fighting for dominance. We feel comfortable conserving our energy with our desks in rows and our students reading their textbooks.

But growth requires discomfort, even pain. Creating and maintaining a complex system requires work and sacrifice. Our society today is facing major challenges that will require individuals and institutions to make hard choices in order to survive. We must teach a set of values to our children that will help them make wise choices in a multicultural world. We must develop their capacities for observing, reasoning, and responding so they can manage a rapidly changing world. We must give them a foundation of values that will let them choose wisely among the technological options now available, and we must reshape our institutions to meet a changing world while responding to the needs of our children.

References

Azuela, M. (1992). *The underdogs* (F. H. Fornoff, Trans.). Pittsburgh, PA: University of Pittsburgh Press.

Bak, P. (1996). *How nature works: The science of self-organized criticality.* New York: Springer-Verlag.

Beard, L. (Ed). (1992). *CHART Directors meeting report.* (CHART Archives, available from International Education Consortium, 13157 Olive Spur Road, St. Louis, MO 63141.)

Benedict, R. (1976). Synergy. In B. Stanford (Ed.), *Peacemaking: A guide to conflict resolution for individuals, groups and nations.* New York: Bantam.

Briggs, J., & Peat, F. D. (1989). *Turbulent mirrors: An illustrated guide to chaos theory and the science of wholeness.* New York: Harper and Row.

Brouillette, L. (1996). *A geology of school reform: The successive restructurings of a school district.* Albany: State University of New York Press.

Caine, R. M., & Caine G. (1997). *Education on the edge of possibility.* Alexandria, VA: Association for Supervision and Curriculum Development.

Chittister, J. (1990). *Wisdom distilled from the daily: Living the rule of St. Benedict today.* San Francisco: Harper.

Comer, J. P. (1992). *For children's sake: The Comer school development program: Discussion leader's guide.* New Haven, CT: Yale Child Study Center.

Copeland, N. D. (1989). *Managing conflict: A curriculum for adolescents.* Albuquerque: New Mexico Center for Dispute Resolution.

Darling-Hammond, L. (1995, Spring/Summer). The school and the democratic community. *The Record,* p. 36.

Davis, B. M. (1994). A cultural safari: Dispelling myths and creating connections through multicultural and international education. *English Journal, 83*(2), 24-26.

Eibl-Eibesfeldt, I. (1979). *Love and hate: The natural history of behavior patterns.* New York: Holt, Rinehart & Winston.

Fosnot, C. T. (1996). Constructivism: A psychological theory of learning. In C. T. Fosnot (Ed.), *Constructivism: Theory, perspectives, and practice.* New York: Teachers College Press.

Fuentes, C. (1991). *The death of Artemio Cruz* (A. MacAdam, Trans). New York: Farrar, Straus & Giroux.

Fullan, M. G. (1993). *Change forces: Probing the depths of educational reform.* London: Falmer.

Fullan, M. G., with Stiegelbauer, S. (1991). *The new meaning of educational change* (2nd ed.). New York: Teachers College Press.

Gleick, J. (1987). *Chaos: Making a new science.* New York: Penguin.

Goleman, D. (1995). *Emotional intelligence.* New York: Bantam.

Gregoire, N., & Prigogine, I. (1989). *Exploring complexity: An introduction.* New York: Freeman.

Hargreaves, A. (1994). *Changing teachers, changing times: Teachers' work and culture in the postmodern age.* London: Cassell.

Henry, W. A., III. (1990). Beyond the melting pot. *Time, 135*(15), 28.

Howard, K. (1993). Portfolio culture in Pittsburgh. In R. Jennings (Ed.), *Fire in the eyes of youth.* St. Paul, MN: Occasional Press.

Inhabiting other lives: A humanities project. (c. 1992). Unpublished report on the Miami project. (CHART Archives, available from International Education Consortium, 13157 Olive Spur Road, St. Louis, MO 63141.)

Javers, R. (1994). *A change of mind.* New York: Rockefeller Foundation.

Kauffman, S. (1993). *The origins of order: Self-organization and selection in evolution.* New York: Oxford University Press.

Kauffman, S. (1995). *At home in the universe: The search for laws of self-organization and complexity.* New York: Oxford University Press.

Kiely, K. (1995, July 31). Public education budget woes sour governors' forum. *Arkansas Democrat-Gazette,* p. A7.

Kordsmeier, J. (1997, June 6). Dip in violence drops LR out of bloody top 20. *Arkansas Democrat Gazette,* p. 1A.

Lewin, R. (1992). *Complexity: Life at the edge of chaos.* New York: Collier.

Maeroff, G. (1988). *The empowerment of teachers.* New York: Teachers College Press.

Mehlinger, H. D. (1996, February). School reform in the information age. *Phi Delta Kappan, 77*(6), 400-407.

Outlaw, L. (1991). *First seminar on education for a diverse society.* Unpublished CHART paper. (CHART Archives, available from

International Education Consortium, 13157 Olive Spur Road, St. Louis, MO 63141.)

Paz, O. (1961). *The labyrinth of solitude*. New York: Grove.

Prigogine, I., Gregoire, N., & Babloyants, A. (1972a, November). Thermodynamics of evolution, Part I. *Physics Today*, 23-28.

Prigogine, I., Gregoire, N. & Babloyants, A. (1972b, December). Thermodynamics of evolution, Part II. *Physics Today*, 38-41.

Prigogine, I., & Stengers, I. (1984). *Order out of chaos*. New York: Bantam.

Roth, S. (1995, March 5). Under the gun in the hood. *Arkansas Democrat-Gazette*, p. 1A.

Rubinsky, C. (1993). Reflection on writing. In R. Jennings (Ed.), *Fire in the eyes of youth* (pp. 95-97). St. Paul, MN: Occasional Press.

Sadalla, G., Henriquez, M., & Holmberg, M. (n.d.). *Conflict resolution: A secondary school curriculum*. San Francisco: Community Board Program.

Sarason, S. B. (1990). *The predictable failure of educational reform*. San Francisco: Jossey-Bass.

Schlechty, P. C. (1997). *Inventing better schools: An action plan for educational reform*. San Francisco: Jossey-Bass.

Senge, P. M. (1990). *The fifth discipline*. Garden City, NY: Doubleday.

Shack, R. (1992). Welcome. In J. Rényi (Ed.), *Diversified assessment in social studies: Proceedings of the CHART Directors' Meeting*, held in Miami.

Stanford, G. (1990). *Developing effective classroom groups: A practical guide for teachers*. Bristol, UK: Acora.

Stanford, G., & Roark, A. (1974). *Human interaction in education*. Boston: Allyn & Bacon.

Wadsworth, B. J. (1978). *Piaget for the classroom teacher*. New York: Longman.

Waldrop, M. M. (1992). *Complexity: The emerging science at the edge of order and chaos*. New York: Simon & Schuster.

Wallenstein, N. (1987). Problem-posing education: Freire's method for transformation. In I. Shor (Ed.), *Freire in the classroom*. Portsmouth, NH: Boynton/Cook.

Wolf, D. P. (1987/1988). Opening up assessment. *Educational Leadership*, 26-27.

Index

CORWIN PRESS

The Corwin Press logo—a raven striding across an open book— represents the happy union of courage and learning. We are a professional-level publisher of books and journals for K–12 educators, and we are committed to creating and providing resources that embody these qualities. Corwin's motto is "Success for All Learners."